Confidence

Prentice Hall LIFE

If life is what you make it, then making it better starts here.

What we learn today can change our lives tomorrow. It can change our goals or change our minds; open up new opportunities or simply inspire us to make a difference. That's why we have created a new breed of books that do more to help you make more of *your* life.

Whether you want more confidence or less stress, a new skill or a different perspective, we've designed *Prentice Hall Life* books to help you to make a change for the better. Together with our authors we share a commitment to bring you the brightest ideas and best ways to manage your life, work and wealth.

In these pages we hope you'll find the ideas you need for the life *you* want. Go on, help yourself.

It's what you make it

* * *

Confidence

The art of getting whatever you want

Rob Yeung

Harlow, England • London • New York • Boston • San Francisco • Toronto • Sydney • Singapore • Hong Kong
Tokyo • Seoul • Taipei • New Delhi • Cape Town • Madrid • Mexico City • Amsterdam • Munich • Paris • Milan

PEARSON EDUCATION LIMITED

Edinburgh Gate
Harlow CM20 2JE
Tel: +44 (0)1279 623623
Fax: +44 (0)1279 431059
Website: www.pearsoned.co.uk

First published in Great Britain in 2008

© Pearson Education 2008

The right of Rob Yeung to be identified as author of this work has been asserted by him in accordance with the Copyright, Designs and Patents Act 1988.

ISBN: 978-0-273-71513-9

British Library Cataloguing-in-Publication Data
A catalogue record for this book is available from the British Library

Library of Congress Cataloging-in-Publication Data
Yeung, Rob.
   Confidence : the art of getting whatever you want / Rob Yeung. -- 1st ed.
      p. cm.
   ISBN 978-0-273-71513-9
   1. Self-confidence. I. Title.
   BF575.S39Y48 2008
   158--dc22
                                    2008021585

10 9 8 7 6 5 4 3 2 1
12 11 10 09 08

Typeset in 10pt IowanOldStyle by 3
Printed and bound in Great Britain by Ashford Colour Press Ltd, Gosport, Hants

The Publisher's policy is to use paper manufactured from sustainable forests.

Contents

About the author

Psychologist and coach Dr Rob Yeung helps people to achieve their goals. He presents at conferences, consults to organisations and coaches individuals. Known for his inspiring and informative style, he helps people to make positive changes in their lives and achieve success.

As an international speaker, he addresses audiences ranging from business leaders and entrepreneurs to sales people and college students. As an author, he has written over a dozen books which have been translated into many languages around the world. A popular expert on television, he appears on everything from CNN to *Big Brother*, and as the presenter of programmes including *How To Get Your Dream Job* for the BBC.

He trained as an exercise and sports psychologist and is a chartered psychologist of the British Psychological Society. And he's a qualified personal trainer and aerobics instructor too.

For more information, visit: www.robyeung.com.

Acknowledgements

Thanks to my parents for their unwavering confidence that I can achieve whatever I set my mind to. To my Talentspace colleagues for being there. To Steve Cuthbertson for creating the eye in the sometimes stormy world I inhabit. To Bonnie Chiang and Mandy Wheeler for their comments. To my editor Sam Jackson for her ongoing support.

Introduction

Want to transform your life and have astounding levels of confidence? The good news is that you can. Because no matter how much or how little confidence you have, you can always have more.

It's a myth that most people are confident. In fact, *many* people report that they would like to feel more confident. People who appear confident may still feel nervous inside. People who are confident at work may be shy when it comes to dating; people who are confident at parties may feel panicky giving presentations. So if you would like to be more confident, you're in good company.

Confidence is not something that you are born either with or without. Confidence is not an all-or-nothing personality trait that you're stuck with for life. We are all capable of feeling more confident. We can nurture and develop our confidence at any age by adopting new behaviours and strategies. Best of all, you already have all of the resources that you need – my job in writing this book is to help you to discover those resources within yourself.

Maybe you are looking to develop your confidence in your personal life or at work. Perhaps you just need more confidence in a particular situation such as speaking in front of an audience or facing up to a colleague, asking someone on a date, or making an impact during interviews. Or maybe you crave more confidence in several areas of your life. You may be only mildly worried by certain situations or stricken by paralysing fears. From the boardroom to the bedroom, this book is filled with proven techniques and exercises for boosting your confidence.

This stuff works!

To help you become your best, most confident self, I have packed this book with techniques, tips, and scientifically proven exercises. I have drawn on the best from fields including cognitive behavioural therapy, sport psychology, neuro-linguistic programming, and positive psychology. Some of this stuff is so cutting-edge you could get paper cuts simply turning the pages. Don't worry if that sounds like so much gobbledygook – take it on trust that I've scoured the worlds of academia, business, and life coaching to bring you only stuff that works.

That's because I have been frustrated in recent years that there are books on confidence that simply do not deliver results. I'm afraid there are frauds and quacks who tout fluffy, frivolous ideas that do not have a lasting impact on confidence. Sure, some of their techniques may feel good for days or even weeks – but do they deliver long-term benefits? No. Well this book is different.

Take note throughout the book of one-off 'Take Action' exercises, as well as 'Confidence Booster' techniques that you will want to use again and again. Using these, you will learn not only how to project a more confident image but also how to change the way you think and feel about yourself and the world. The result? You will build a profound and lasting confidence to deal with just about anything that life could throw at you. If you put your trust in Dr Rob, I won't let you down.

A personal story

I wholeheartedly believe that confidence can be built. And I speak as both a psychologist and someone who used to suffer from crippling fears. When I was younger, I was so petrified of public speaking to even a handful of people that I felt physically sick – I literally used to retch as if I were going to throw up. I was so scared that I used to pretend I was ill to get out of doing it. But I've since trained myself to love speaking to audiences of many hundreds of people at a time. And as I sometimes appear on TV, on programmes ranging from BBC shows to CNN news and *Big Brother*, I now get the biggest buzz from being in the spotlight on live television in front of millions of people.

But I wouldn't say that I'm anything special. I'm an ordinary person who used to suffer from a lack of confidence but applied some techniques to boost it. My message: if I can do it, so can you.

Get involved

By using this book, you'll learn how to lift your confidence quickly. No matter what your state of mind, I guarantee that investing a few minutes every day on the tools within this book will act like a shot of steroids to your confidence. Almost immediately, you will feel more relaxed and energised. And in the long-term you will develop such unassailable levels of jut-jawed confidence that you will be able to handle just about *anything*.

BUT – and here's the but – to get the most out of this book, you can't just read it and set it aside. You have to *do* the exercises and *use* the techniques. This book can transform your levels of confidence and help you to achieve a more satisfying and successful life. But only if you put in the work! A football coach trains and advises a team but ultimately has to trust the players to deliver on the football field. So think of me as your confidence coach. My job is to offer you the latest in scientifically proven techniques and exercises. But you are the one who has to go out on the football pitch of your own life.

Feel free to work through this book at your own pace. Whether you want to race through it all at once, take the journey more leisurely, or flick backwards and forwards between interesting chapters, the choice is yours. But reading and appreciating how the ideas in this book might work for people in general is not the same as applying them in your own life. So make sure you do the fun interactive activities and exercises. You need to do the thinking, put pen to paper, take action.

Understanding the principles is not the same as using them. So each time you come across an exercise, please complete it before you move on. Each time you learn a new technique, find the time to use it in your everyday life. The more you participate with this book, refer to it, scribble your thoughts in the margins, highlight passages that jump out at you, and note techniques you want to try again and again, the more your confidence will swell. Don't just read – get involved.

Life-long confidence *and* immediate needs

I've divided this book into two parts. Part 1 takes you on a journey to build a sense of confidence that will see you through the rest of your life. You will understand how to enhance your confidence, no matter how little of it you currently have. You will work through exercises to open your eyes to untapped strengths and personal resources. You will learn tricks to apply in all sorts of situations, not only to appear more self-assured but also to create a confident mindset.

Part 2 is different because it tackles in greater detail the common situations that many people find daunting. Perhaps you need to stand up and speak in front of a crowd or wow interviewers and get yourself a new job. Maybe you want to fuel your confidence before meeting new people at a party or at work. Or you may be thinking of making a change in your life.

If any of that applies to you, Part 2 will help you to get what you want.

Time to get started

I would wish you good luck, but you don't need luck. Your fate is within your control. Success depends only on your decision to use the tools within this book. Do the work and you will gain the confidence. It really is that simple. So enjoy the book and drop me an email to let me know how you get on.

Anyway, are you ready to get going? Let's kick off our journey to craft the new, more confident you.

Dr Rob Yeung
rob@robyeung.com

Part 1

Developing life-long confidence

01

Confidence and you

"What the mind can conceive, the mind can achieve."

Clement Stone, entrepreneur and philanthropist

In this chapter you will...

- learn what confidence is and what it can allow you to achieve
- understand that you can take control of your life, no matter what's going on around you right now
- discover how your thoughts and behaviour influence how you feel about yourself
- measure your current levels of confidence and uncover the areas of your life that most need changing
- look at your strengths and start the positive journey to creating a more confident life.

So what comes to mind when we talk about confidence? Perhaps you think of confidence as how people behave. Think of the confident folks you know and maybe you imagine how they laugh and smile, give unwavering presentations or seem to ace job interviews. Or you see them mingling with strangers, acting larger-than-life, and happily being the centre of attention.

But how people come across is only a part of being confident. Most of what makes up confidence is what confidence allows you to *achieve*. Because there are people who are quietly confident – who don't draw attention to themselves but manage to conquer life's challenges and get what they want from life.

And that's what confidence is mainly about – allowing people to achieve their goals. Because confident people:

- deal with new situations, difficulties and opportunities – seeing them as challenges to be tackled and overcome rather than threats to be avoided
- take responsibility for making change happen rather than wishing their circumstances or the people around them would change

- realise that, while they can't always control what happens to them, they can always control how they respond
- move outside of their comfort zones to try new experiences – they feel anxiety, worry, and fear but push on regardless in order to achieve their long-term goals
- cope with setbacks by putting more effort into achieving what they want – even when they feel downhearted and are thinking of giving up
- learn from mistakes and look for ways to move on rather than letting setbacks get them down
- have a sense of purpose and set both long- and short-term goals to pursue what they want from life.

Interested? Does any of that sound appealing?

As you can see from the list, confidence is not always about feeling good inside. Yes, confident people can feel self-assured and good about themselves. But they sometimes feel scared or overwhelmed too. Confident people can still feel anxious about important projects at work or by troubles in their personal lives. The difference between confident people and less confident people is not in how much they *feel* fear or anxiety, but in how confident people put up with those feelings and deal with their situations regardless.

Okay, so that's what confidence allows people – and that includes you – to do. But what is confidence exactly? And how can you get more of it?

Confidence is about action

Let's define confidence. I say that confidence is 'the ability to take appropriate and effective action, however challenging it may feel at the time'. Confidence is about doing what you need to do in the short-term to achieve your long-term goals, even if what you need to do in the short-term may feel temporarily uncomfortable.

Sure, you may feel scared by a task or situation. But becoming confident is about learning to manage those feelings in order to achieve your long-term goals. Say you're worried about going for job interviews; you will do it anyway because your goal is to find a better job. If you're anxious about speaking in public, you will grit your teeth and do it because it will further your career. If you shy away from meeting new people, taking exams, coping with rejection, asserting yourself, beginning or ending relationships, or whatever else it may be, you will train yourself to do so because it will enhance your long-term happiness.

You'd be surprised how many famous people still get anxious. In a recent interview, legendary singer Dame Shirley Bassey admitted: 'I get more nervous now about going on stage than I ever did.' But that hasn't stopped her from performing to theatres packed with thousands of people or even millions on live television.

I recently coached an international rugby player – one of the England team who won the Rugby World Cup in 2003. Known for being super-cool on the pitch, he was worried about standing up and giving speeches to even smallish groups of business people. But despite his nerves, he was determined to become a successful public speaker.

And you know what? The more you throw yourself into situations that scare you, the more likely you are to enjoy them. At some point, you will forget that you're scared and actually start to feel exhilarated, alive, liberated by what you're doing. I used to be scared of speaking in public. But with practice I overcame my fears. I stopped being scared and I started to love public speaking.

"Courage is resistance to fear, mastery of fear – not absence of fear."

Mark Twain, writer

Over to you

What made you pick this book up? If confidence is about action, start by scribbling your aims on a sheet of paper or even in the margin of this book. Write a couple of sentences that capture what you'd like to get out of this book: in what ways would you like to be more confident? To get you started, here's a list of common situations in which many people feel they could be more confident.

Taking a driving test	Being more assertive
Asking someone out on a date	Speaking in public
Pursuing opportunities and taking risks	Changing career
Handling criticism	Making new friends
Learning a new skill	Coping with rejection
Beginning or ending a relationship	Asking for a pay rise
Dealing with colleagues or customers	Changing your life
Impressing at job interviews	Taking an exam or test
Leaving a bad situation	Receiving compliments
Networking at conferences	Being a parent
Recovering from a trauma	Learning to say 'no' to people
Losing weight or getting fitter	Overcoming fears or worries

Take control, don't be controlled

I want to get across a key message right now: confidence is about taking action, taking control. A lot of people who want more confidence *wish* that their lives would change. They wish their boss were more helpful, their spouse more caring. They wish they had more time or money. They wish they had done something differently in the past or that someone would give them the chance.

But unless you have a reliable genie or a fairy godmother on call, wishing is not a strategy. Your boss is unlikely to become more helpful spontaneously – you either need to work around them or find a different job with a more helpful boss. If you don't have enough time or money (and who does, these days?), then it's up to you to free up a bit more time or set aside a bit of extra cash. If you don't make it happen, it ain't gonna happen by itself.

I beg you: please don't play the wishing game! If you've been wishing, waiting, hoping in the past, that's fine. But seize the moment now. Rather than waiting any longer for your circumstances to change and grant you more confidence, why not go out and grab it?

I'm sure you have heard of people who triumphed over severe adversity. People who suffered extreme poverty, cruelty and abuse, physical disability or crippling illness, and still managed to overcome their difficulties and succeed. They could have wallowed in their misfortunes and complained 'If only my parents hadn't neglected me' or 'If only I hadn't been struck down with cancer'. But they didn't. And the message to take from them is that you *can* succeed no matter what your circumstances. Many people have gruelling backgrounds but still manage to elevate themselves from them. And if *you* want to improve and grow, you can. Be captain of your own destiny. Simply decide to take action.

Think about your own situation for a moment. What constraints are holding you back right now? Perhaps a lack of time, a difficult situation at home, or an uncaring boss? A tough childhood or a lack of education? Not enough money, a bout of ill-health or a lack of fitness? Rather than seeing these as insurmountable barriers stopping you from becoming more confident, you can see them as challenges to be overcome.

"Every man is the architect of his own fortune."

Proverb

Being scared can't kill you

Of course you may be scared at the thought of having to tackle your fears head-on. However, bear in mind that feelings are not reality. Your worries may loom larger than life and cause you a lot of grief – but your worries are only a trick played on you by your own mind. Feeling worried, anxious, scared, frightened, sad, or whatever else you may feel, won't kill you. We are lucky in the modern world that most of the things that frighten us aren't actually fatal. In fact, the worst that can happen is rarely as bad as your imagination suggests.

Over to you

Think about your own experience:

▧ What's the scariest thing you have ever done?

▧ How did it turn out?

You might have been really worried in the run-up to an exam, a talk, or a crucial meeting. Maybe you did something knee-tremblingly terrifying such as a bungee jump for charity. You may have suffered sleepless nights beforehand and incredible nerves on the big day. But how did it go? Probably not as badly as you thought it would. And the fact that you're reading this book means that you lived to tell the tale!

The cycle of confidence

Okay, we've established that confidence is about taking action and taking control. But what exactly are you taking control of? The answer: what you *do*, *think*, and *feel*.

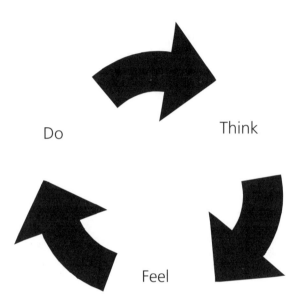

Do Think

Feel

Psychologists have known for a long time that what you *feel*, *do*, and *think* are linked in a cycle, a continuous loop. Suppose someone *feels* nervous about going to a party on her own. So what she *does* is stay at home. Which makes her *think* that she will be lonely forever, making her *feel* unhappy and even less confident about future parties.

Or someone *thinks* he is a loser. By thinking he's a loser, he *feels* unhappy, making him even less likely to *do* anything. He can't muster up the energy to try new things and ends up proving himself right that he's a loser.

If you let your feelings get the better of you, you create a vicious cycle, a self-perpetuating loop that reinforces your fears and drains your confidence.

On the other hand, if you *think* differently, you *feel* differently, and *do* differently. Force yourself to *think* more positively and you start to *feel* happy and confident. Which gives you the kick you need to *do* something new, which in turn reinforces your positive thinking and feelings. And so it goes round again, creating a virtuous cycle that grows your confidence.

The absolutely fantastic news is that you can develop your confidence by intervening at any of the three stages. For example, let's start with the doing. If you behave ('do') as if you are already confident – going to that party, giving a presentation at work, asking someone out on a date – you make it easier for yourself to believe ('think') that you can be confident. In turn, thinking more positively helps you to be ('feel') more relaxed and confident, which helps you to do even more. If you follow the steps in this book by changing your behaviour and ways of thinking, the confidence will come.

Assessing where you are now

Before we look at how to change, let's look at what needs changing. How confident do you feel at the moment?

Read through the following statements and decide how much you agree with each one. Bear in mind that this quiz is for your own use, so be honest. If you score yourself higher than you really feel, you only kid yourself. To work out your score on the self-confidence scale, use the following scoring guide:

1	2	3	4	5
'disagree strongly'	'disagree slightly'	'neither agree nor disagree'	'agree slightly'	'agree strongly'

The Self-Confidence Scale

Statement	1	2	3	4	5
I always manage to solve difficult problems if I try hard enough.					
If people oppose me, I can find ways to achieve what I want.					
I find it easy to stick to my aims and achieve my goals.					
I am resourceful enough to handle unforeseen situations in all of the different areas of my life.					
I am confident that I can deal effectively with unexpected events and setbacks.					
I usually find several solutions to the problems I encounter.					
I remain calm when faced with difficulties in both my personal and professional life.					
I can solve most of the problems I am confronted with.					
I put more effort into my work when things aren't going well because I want to achieve my goals.					
I am certain that I can handle whatever comes my way.					

Understanding your rating

Now add up your scores from the 10 statements to get an overall score between 10 and 50. What do the scores on the doors say about you?

■ **Score of between 41 and 50**: You are a confident person who believes firmly in your abilities to overcome difficulties, solve problems, and succeed even in the face of adversity. Scan through the book and choose the handful of Take Action exercises and Confidence Booster techniques that will help you to maintain your high levels of confidence.

■ **Score of between 31 and 40**: You are confident most of the time in your ability to deal with the situations and impasses that you encounter. Like most people, you may be more confident in some areas of your life than others. Work through the Take Action exercises and explore which of the Confidence Boosters could help you to improve your confidence just that little bit more.

■ **Score of between 21 and 30**: Your confidence could be somewhat higher. Perhaps you are feeling a little anxious or experiencing some uncertainty about how to deal with your circumstances. But using the Confidence Boosters and Take Action exercises will help you to develop both day-to-day and longer-term confidence.

■ **Score of between 10 and 20**: Your confidence seems to be rather low at the moment, but we can work on that. In fact, the lower your confidence, the easier it is to make quick progress. Start with the Confidence Boosters in Chapter 2 to change your beliefs, your view of life. But don't take too much on at once – make sure you become familiar with each technique and have incorporated it into your life before you move on to the next one.

Once you have totalled up your score, take a note of it right now. Maybe jot your score in the margin of this book along with today's date. Irrespective of your score today, you will see your confidence grow as you use the tools in this book. Come back to complete the test again in six months' time and you are certain to record much higher scores.

Seven spheres of a confident life

Most of us live at such a furious pace that we don't get the chance to ask ourselves how we're doing and what we want from life. Well this is your chance now.

The questionnaire you just completed looks at how much confidence you have at the moment. And I know I've already asked you to think of certain situations that you would like to have more confidence in. But sometimes people need confidence in ways that are to do less with specific situations and more with broader areas of their lives. And that's what this next exercise sets out to measure.

Look at the seven spheres of a confident life and score your level of confidence in each on a scale of 1 to 10. A '10' represents incredibly high levels of confidence – you are not only totally satisfied with how you feel in this area of your life, but other people probably look on in astonishment at what you have achieved in it too. A '1' score represents very low levels of confidence – you're deeply unhappy with this area of your life.

Remember that, as with all of the exercises in this book, the results are for you alone. No one else sees them, so be honest in how you rate the different areas of your life. Put a tick in each box to represent your satisfaction with each area.

The seven spheres of a confident life are as follows:

- **Your physical life.** Consider your confidence in your physical health, fitness, diet, energy levels, and well-being. Are you concerned with your health? Do you feel strong and healthy all of the time or do you have aches and pains, coughs and colds? A '10' score implies you're someone who springs out of bed in the mornings with boundless energy, confident in the knowledge that you will be able to take on anything during the course of the day and still have the energy to do more during the evening until you decide to go to bed. A lower score implies you often feel tired, ill, or that you could look after yourself better.

- **Your intimate life.** Think about your level of confidence in the relationship with your partner, spouse, or significant other. Think about your partner right now: does your partner support you, make you laugh and feel loved, bring you joy and happiness? A high level of confidence means that you are deeply satisfied with your relationship. Or, if you do not have a partner, you may still score this area highly if you are completely happy as an independent person. A low score means that you could feel a lot happier – either because you wish you could improve the quality of your existing relationship or because you yearn to be with someone.

- **Your family life.** Think about your relationships with your parents, any siblings, children, and the wider family. Do you feel totally loved and supported by your family? Do you feel confident enough to be yourself with them? How much confidence do you generally feel when dealing with your family?

- **Your social life.** How confident do you feel about your social life? Do you see your friends as much as you would like? Do they get in touch with you often enough? Do you have the confidence to meet new people and make new friends? A high score implies that your social life exceeds your expectations. A low score may mean that you would like to be more confident in your relationships with your friends.

- **Your occupational life.** Consider how confident you feel at work. To what extent do you feel fulfilled and thrilled by your work? Do you feel confident that your work allows you to express the person you want to be? A high score implies that you are happy with the nature of your work, your prospects, and the relationships you have at work. However, if you consider your work to be a chore that you do only to pay the bills, you may wish to score this area lower.

■ **Your financial life**. Consider your confidence in your ability to *manage* your money. How confident are you that you are able to provide for yourself and your loved ones? That you are able to pay the bills and put something aside? Most of us could easily do with a little more money, but this sphere is not about how much money you have. Some people earn millions but still worry about having enough. Others earn very little and yet live contentedly within their means. How much confidence do you have in your ability to manage your finances and feel secure with the money you have?

■ **Your sense of purpose in life**. Confident people have a sense of purpose and meaning in their lives. They feel confident that they have tasks to perform in their time on Earth – they give freely of their time, energy, and other resources without expectation of anything in return. Others lack that confidence and certainty, drifting from one day to the next. People who score highly on this sphere often get involved with causes such as community groups, charities, their faith or religion, society, the environment, and so on. In what ways do you contribute to the wider world? How confident are you that you live a meaningful life?

I have left three lines of the table blank for you to add any further areas of your life that are important to you. For example, some people crave recognition for their efforts or have a faith that they need to follow. You are unique and may have your own areas that you need to pay attention to in order to feel satisfied and fulfilled in your whole life. So before you read on, consider: what else might be really essential to you in your life and need capturing in the table opposite?

When you've scored the seven spheres of your life, give yourself a pat on the back. So many people live their lives feeling anything from slightly dissatisfied to downright miserable and yet do nothing about it. But not you. By rating the level of confidence you have in the different areas of your life, you are putting

Scoring the seven spheres of a confident life

	1	2	3	4	5	6	7	8	9	10
Your physical life										
Your intimate life										
Your family life										
Your social life										
Your occupational										
life										
Your financial life										
Your sense of										
purpose in life										

a stake in the ground, making a commitment to yourself, and giving yourself a good shot at changing your prospects.

Once you've put your ticks in the different boxes, consider *why* you've given yourself these scores. Give each sphere a little thought. Write a few notes on what is going on in that sphere of your life. For each sphere, use the following questions to prompt your thinking:

■ What is *good* that is currently happening?

■ What is *bad* and could do with changing?

■ What is *new* that you would like to see develop?

If they can do it ...

Alison is a 31-year-old supervisor at an insurance company. She works long hours and feels constantly drained – her first waking thoughts are often of work and she returns every evening with work still spinning in her head. Feeling that her life is slipping away, she reviews the seven spheres of her life. She gives herself high scores in her occupational and financial life and is reasonably content with some of the other areas of her life. She gives herself the lowest scores – 3 out of 10 in both cases – on her intimate life and sense of purpose in life.

She writes a paragraph on each of the seven spheres, including the following on the two that she scores lowest in.

■ **In my intimate life:** I have plenty of friends, but I don't have a relationship in my life. I have plenty of single women friends, so the pressure doesn't feel on to find a partner. But I am sometimes lonely. I'm so busy at work – but do I use my work as an excuse not to meet someone? I have friends who have tried internet dating but I'm too embarrassed to give it a go – I don't want anyone to feel that I'm desperate. On the other hand, I haven't made much progress in recent years. And the fact that I've scored this sphere as a 3 must mean that it's more important to me than I let on even to myself.

■ **My sense of purpose in life:** What is my purpose in life? I do think that I'd love to do something for a charity. Whenever I see that advert for the children's charity on TV, I get all these ideas into my head. But then the daily grind of projects at work brings me back down to earth so quickly. I know no one on their death bed ever wishes they'd spent more time in the office. But what do I really want to do? I'm not sure. I've never had the time – or perhaps more accurately I've never made the time – but maybe I need to find out.

Having invested the time in reviewing the different spheres of her life, Alison commits to giving these two key areas more thought. She picks out a Saturday later in the month and is determined to work through some more exercises and activities then.

You can write as little or as much as you like about the different spheres of your life. Some people find that a few bullet points are enough; other people write a few paragraphs on certain spheres, but pages on other spheres. Do what works for you.

We're going to leave this exercise for now. But we'll come back to it later on when we come to putting together a vision for your new, more confident life.

Get ready to succeed

Invest in a good quality notebook, journal or binder that you will be proud to use. You can write your thoughts in it and keep track of your progress as you work through the exercises in this book. By keeping all your reflections in one place, you can refer to them easily in future. And when you come to look back on them, you will quickly be able to see how much progress you have made.

Celebrating your strengths

So far we have focused on the areas where you may not feel entirely confident. But let's now look at the areas where you are strong. We all have unique strengths and we all perform more confidently when we can play to those strengths.

Imagine a football team with a great centre forward and a superb goalkeeper. What would happen if the team manager put the goalkeeper into the centre forward position and the centre forward into goal? Can you imagine how the two players would perform? Badly, almost certainly. Do you suppose that the two players would feel confident in their new roles? No, probably not.

People are more successful *and* confident when they focus on their strengths rather than dwell on their weaknesses. I'm sure you know from personal experience that investing your energies in an activity you are good at is much more fun than working on one of your hated weaknesses. Off the top of your head, what are the tasks you hate doing? And what stuff do you get a kick out of?

Many people downplay their talents. But just because a talent comes naturally to you does not mean that it comes easily to others. Perhaps you pick up foreign languages quickly. Maybe you impress friends and family with your cooking. Or are you the technology whiz who is always sorting out everyone else's computers, or the sympathetic ear whenever people have problems? Whatever your talents, you probably feel knowledgeable, strong, and in control when you deploy them.

No one can be good at everything. And confident people know that they need to give themselves credit for their strengths rather than beat themselves up for their weaknesses. You don't think David Beckham gives himself a hard time for not being a good goalie, do you? If your life is a game of football, let's identify your strengths and figure out what position would best suit you.

"The same man cannot be well skilled in everything; each has his own special excellence."

Euripedes, Greek dramatist

Over to you

Here are the beginnings of two statements:

■ I am good at . . . .

■ I enjoy . . . .

Copy them out and complete them *at least* 10 times each – yes, 10.

Most people are too modest about their strengths so you may need to overcome your overly humble nature. Think about all of the different areas of your life. Your strengths may lie in how you handle people, numbers, facts, animals, plans, food, technology, ideas, fashion, yourself, or anything else you can think of. Capture every strength that comes to mind – no matter how mundane or trivial you think it may be. Once you've written down all of your statements, have a look back at them. What do you see?

Give it a shot right now. Take just five minutes to complete the sentence stems on a fresh sheet of paper. Soon you'll find new strengths tumbling out of your head. But if you get stuck for inspiration, why not get your family and friends to help? Meet for a coffee, pick up the telephone, or drop them an email to explain that you've taken on a personal development project. Ask them: 'What do you think I'm good at?'

I'm willing to bet that your friends and family are more positive about what you can do than you are about yourself. So it won't be long before you have plenty of ideas about your strengths.

When you have more time, try this next exercise too.

Take Action: Telling the story of your strengths

Being able to use your strengths regularly will help you to be successful as well as satisfied. However, we can sometimes get side-tracked into different avenues that take us away from our strengths; people often find that they felt most fulfilled at some earlier stage in their lives. So this story-telling exercise enables you to track down strengths you may have forgotten you have.

Start by figuring out the year when you were 10 years old. If you were born in 1967, you were 10 in 1977.

1 **Outline what happened to you that year.** Remind yourself where you lived, who you spent time with, and what you spent most of your time doing.

2 **List your personal successes for that year.** Write down every success you achieved. Keep your definition of success as broad as possible to include everything you accomplished, were responsible for, overcame, or were proud of – no matter how large or small. You only need to write a couple of words or a sentence on each at this stage. But aim for at least two or three successes for the year.

3 **Then move on to the next year.** Go back to step 1 and 2 for every year of your life until you catch up with the present day.

4 **Pull out the personal successes you *enjoyed* achieving.** For each success that you took pleasure from, write a paragraph describing what you did. Write in the first person ('I did . . .') as if you are telling a friend the story of what you did. Focus mainly on the actions and decisions you took – what you did, said, and made happen – that turned the situation into a success.

5 **Look at the *verbs* in your stories.** Look at the decisions you made and the actions you took. What talents did you exercise to achieve each success? Your strengths could be anything. You may feel strong when listening to other people, making others feel valued, analysing problems, working with animals, understanding technology, making plans, or showing integrity. Perhaps you feel strong when creating with your hands, inspiring others, negotiating deals, demonstrating empathy, challenging the status quo, serving others, and so on.

This exercise will take a bit of time, but it's worth doing. Remember that much of the value of this book is in the doing, not the reading. Sure, you understand the concept of identifying your strengths, but understanding is not execution. Only when you know your strengths can you find roles – both in work and outside of it – that will help you to feel most confident.

Understanding your sources of confidence

People may have low confidence for all sorts of reasons – their childhood, their genes, their age, their circumstances. But irrespective of what has happened to you in the past and what is happening to you now, you can influence your future. Building your confidence is like assembling the pieces of a jigsaw. Below are the six pieces of the confidence jigsaw that you will pull together in Part 1 of this book.

- **Your mindset and beliefs.** Confident people have positive beliefs and are optimistic about the situations they encounter. But many people beat themselves up for their mistakes and failings or allow their fears and worries to overwhelm them. Thankfully, psychologists have discovered that people can change the way they think. You can train your mind to develop positive, constructive beliefs and a rugged sense of confidence. I tackle how to do this in Chapter 2.

- **Your goals.** Confident people have goals – they know what they want to achieve in life. They know when to work hard and when to conserve their energies to achieve their goals. People who don't have goals tend to drift in their lives and allow their circumstances to dent their confidence. I share with you how to set effective goals in Chapter 3.

- **Your behaviour.** The *do, think, feel* cycle tells us that if you behave confidently, you can help yourself to think and feel more confident about yourself. I share with you tips and techniques for behaving in ways that will not only make you *appear* more confident but will also make you *feel* more confident. I cover how to do this in Chapter 4.

- **Your resilience.** Confident people bounce back from setbacks and rejection, adversity and criticism. Even if you can't always control everything that happens to you, you can always control how you choose to respond. I talk about how to recover quickly from setbacks in Chapter 5.

■ **Your resources.** Confident people draw upon all manner of resources in developing and maintaining their confidence. They draw upon the support of other people, their environment, and rituals to feel good about themselves. I talk about how to make the most of your resources in Chapter 6.

■ **Your ways to keep going.** Growing your confidence is a marathon, not a sprint. In Chapter 7 I share with you how to review your progress and keep your motivation high.

Feel free to skip ahead to the chapters that most interest you. If, say, you need to behave confidently immediately, then head to Chapter 4. If you want to find out about using your resources, then Chapter 6 is the one for you. But if you would like to come with me on the most effective journey towards the new, more confident you, then let's work through the chapters in order. But before we move on to Chapter 2, congratulate yourself for completing Chapter 1 – your journey to the new, more confident you is well on its way.

ONWARDS AND UPWARDS

■ Confidence is the ability to take action, however challenging it may feel at the time. That may mean feeling a bit scared or anxious but deciding to take action anyway in the knowledge that it will get a heck of a lot easier the next time.

■ Confidence is a quality that *anyone* can get more of. Irrespective of your upbringing or education, or whatever constraints are currently holding you back, you can decide to take practical steps to improve your life and renew your confidence.

■ Remember that feeling worried, anxious, frightened, sad, or scared can't kill you! If your confidence is at a low ebb, you must remember that what you are feeling is only your mind playing tricks on you.

- Remember the *do, think, feel* cycle. If you *do* confidence and *think* confidently, you will quickly *feel* more confident too.

- You may currently lack confidence in only specific situations or in quite broad areas of your life. But it doesn't matter what your current circumstances are. By understanding where you are now, together we can work on getting you where you want to go.

- When you deploy your strengths, you undoubtedly feel in control, strong, and invigorated. So before we move on to Chapter 2 to discuss how you would like your life to be different, take the time to figure out your strengths.

02

Developing bullet-proof beliefs

"They can conquer who believe they can."

John Dryden, playwright

In this chapter you will...

- learn that, while your beliefs have a strong effect on how you feel and behave, they may not always be an accurate reflection of what is going on around you

- come to appreciate that your beliefs and attitude are not permanent – you can choose to change them

- discover tried-and-tested techniques for challenging unhelpful beliefs and replacing them with more helpful ones

- learn to feel motivated and confident by changing the messages you tell yourself and the images you play out in your head

- explore a simple yet proven method for developing your sense of optimism.

Confidence is a mind game. Confidence comes not from being tall or short, a man or a woman, young or old, or any other physical characteristic. Confident people believe in themselves. And because they believe, they achieve.

Take a moment to ask yourself what you believe about yourself. What messages do you generally feed yourself? Do you mainly tell yourself how strong, talented, and confident you are? Or do you lay into yourself about your mistakes, your weaknesses, and your failings?

Whatever your current state of mind, you can quickly improve your confidence by consciously changing how you think about yourself and the world. By using tried-and-tested techniques, you can think more positively, optimistically, and constructively. You can learn to think confidently in the same way that you can learn to ride a bike or play tennis.

Your thoughts matter

The beliefs you hold and the thoughts you have can make you feel strong and excited or tense and unhappy. Some of these beliefs may be long-held and deep-seated, while other messages you tell yourself may be more fleeting but no less damaging to your self-confidence. Tell yourself 'Everyone's going to laugh at me' or 'I'm going to fail' and your self-confidence withers.

"If you think you can or you think you can't – you're right."

Henry Ford, car manufacturer

Remember the *do, think, feel* cycle. If you think that you are capable of achieving more, you feel positive and you become able to do more. If you tell yourself (think) you're a failure, you feel down and ensure you become a failure. Decades of research back me up on this too: you are what you think.

If you've heard of the placebo effect, you know that belief alone can heal the human body. Doctors know that giving a dummy pill with no medicine in it can cure patients with conditions ranging from angina and asthma to headaches and intestinal ulcers. Even when patients unknowingly take empty pill capsules or swallow sugar tablets, their belief that they will get better actually affects their physiologies.

Beliefs are not reality

You are not born with your beliefs, your attitude, your ways of thinking. Your beliefs are influenced not only by what goes on around you but also by what you *choose* to believe.

Different people experiencing exactly the same event can end up with different beliefs. Even though the situation may be the same, their thoughts can go in wildly different directions.

Consider a situation in which six people go for a job interview. They're all interviewed by the managing director, the boss of the business. Unfortunately the boss comes across as cold and unfriendly during the interview. A few days later they all get a letter in the post saying 'It was a pleasure to meet you but I'm afraid that you were not successful in getting the job'. Each person might explain the reason for being rejected in a different way. And because of the *do, think, feel* cycle, how they think about the rejection – the beliefs they hold or the stories they tell themselves – affect their feelings too. Let's look at the six different ways each person thinks and feels.

- Person 1 thinks: 'I'm rubbish at interviews – I should never have gone for this interview.' They feel depressed.

- Person 2 thinks: 'I wouldn't want to work for that company anyway because the boss was so rude!' They feel relieved.

- Person 3 thinks: 'That was a good opportunity for me to practise my interview skills. I will continue to go to interviews and improve each time until I get a job.' This person feels happy.

- Person 4 thinks: 'The interviewer must have hated me.' They feel ashamed.

- Person 5 thinks: 'There must have been another candidate with better experience'. They feel mildly disappointed.

- Person 6 thinks: 'The managing director's letter says that "it was a pleasure" to meet me.' This person feels upbeat and more determined to succeed at the next interview.

Six people, one event. Each person experiences the same situation. The facts for each person are the same. But each person manages to interpret the situation in a different way, leading to a range of different emotions. Some of the emotions damage their confidence; other emotions have little effect or even enhance it.

You must understand: your beliefs are not the same as reality. Yes they *feel* real, but they are only your interpretation, one perspective, on what's going on. Even though you may hold strong beliefs about yourself and your abilities, your beliefs exist because of the way you think – and not because the world is that way.

The voice within

"When you doubt your power, you give power to your doubt."

Anonymous

Imagine for a moment that you have a house guest who keeps telling you how rubbish and stupid you are. From the first thing in the morning, your house guest tells you how foolish you are to consider doing anything new like inviting an attractive person out on a date, asking your boss for a raise, or looking for a new job. Imagine that your guest keeps putting you down all day long, telling you what's wrong with you dozens and dozens of times. And before you fall asleep, your guest reminds you of all the mistakes you've made so that you can relive them all over again.

How would that make you feel? Of course, putting up with someone like that in your life would grate on your nerves and make you miserable. But that's exactly what many of us have.

A guest – not in our house – but in our head who condemns us and makes us feel bad.

We all have an inner voice – experts call it our self-talk. You're probably hearing it right now as you read this sentence. Say hello to your inner voice. Hello!

Your inner voice may speak to you in the first person (e.g. 'I'm really bored right now') or the second person (e.g. 'You need to water the plants before you go on holiday') or switch back and forth between the two. It acts as a running commentary on what you're doing, what you've done, and what you need to be doing. This can be useful in reminding you of stuff you have to do, such as 'The weather forecast said it was going to rain today – I should take an umbrella with me' or 'Remember to get a birthday card for Sarah before the weekend'. But the voice inside your head can also compliment or criticise you. And if you're like most people, you probably don't hear your inner voice making positive comments too often. The voice is more likely to be acting as an inner critic, saying 'That looks really scary', 'Everyone's looking at me', or 'I'm going to fail and look stupid if I give this a go so I'd better not bother trying'.

Experts estimate that we say between 150 and 300 words a minute when we engage in this internal banter. As you can imagine, this can add up to thousands of internal messages every day. Unsurprisingly, your inner critic influences the way you see the world, filtering your experience and shaping your beliefs. It acts as a far harsher judge of you than anyone else could ever be.

If you're not feeling as confident as you could be, your inner critic is probably shooting down your ideas and blaming you for your mistakes. Let's help you to kick out your inner critic and replace it with an inner coach instead.

Consider:

- What messages do you tend to tell yourself?

- Are they mostly positive or negative?

- What kind of messages would you *prefer* to feed yourself?

Creeping in our heads

You probably don't spend a lot of time thinking about the way you think. After all, you've been doing it for as long as you can remember. It just happens, it's automatic. But that can be dangerous. Because negative thoughts can pop into your head from your subconscious without you consciously asking for them. And the more you tell yourself that you're a failure or stupid or whatever else you criticise yourself for, the stronger your beliefs become. And because of the *do, think, feel* cycle, when you think yourself to be stupid or ridiculous or a failure, you start to feel and behave that way to prove yourself right.

Psychologists call the unbidden criticisms that pop into our heads *automatic negative thoughts* (ANTs). They can take many forms, but here are a few examples:

- 'I can't do it – I'm not bright enough to succeed.'

- 'People just don't like me.'

- 'I'll never change – I'm too old and set in my ways.'

- 'Everyone will laugh at me if I mess this up.'

- 'It's too difficult.'

You can rest assured that nearly everyone falls prey to occasional ANTs. Even Olympic athletes and top-flight sports people experience doubts and worries. World-class competitors in tennis, golf, swimming and other disciplines recognise that their physical prowess must be matched by a positive internal dialogue.

And that's what you are going to learn to do. Over four decades of research and practice tell us that you can consciously monitor your thoughts, spot the ANTs for the little monsters that they are, and exterminate them from your head.

Get ready to succeed

Your beliefs have probably developed over the years as a result of your upbringing, religion, culture, class, circumstances, and so on. But you may be pleased to hear that you don't have to worry about where they come from! Twenty-first century psychology tells us that you don't have to dig up the past, dredge up unhappy memories, or revisit old feelings. What happened in your past can stay in the past. To be happier and more confident, you need only live in the present and tackle the thoughts that are bothering you now.

"The greatest discovery of my generation is that people can alter their lives by altering their attitudes of mind."

William James, philosopher

Rallying behind your inner coach

Your inner critic can be a pain in the neck. Take on a new challenge and it whispers: 'This will go horribly wrong', 'You're a fool to expose yourself like this', 'You'll be sorry!' But you can drown it out.

This first Confidence Booster summons forth your inner coach. Perhaps you're getting ready to give a presentation, struggling with a difficult problem, or trying to motivate yourself to do 10 more minutes at the gym. In mere minutes you can arm yourself with a handful of capability-affirming thoughts (CATs) to shout out your automatic negative thoughts (ANTs).

Confidence Booster: Creating your cool CATs

CATs are capability-affirming thoughts. You may have heard people call them positive affirmations or helpful self-talk. Take a moment to jot down constructive statements you could say to yourself when your confidence is threatened. Consider different CATs for different situations. What you tell yourself just before your big speech may differ from what you say when you're trying to motivate yourself to do an extra 10 minutes on the treadmill or when you're struggling with a thorny problem at your desk. Imagine your very own coach standing next to you, rallying you on, motivating you to keep going, encouraging you to be the best you can. Examples include:

- 'Come on, you can do it!'

- 'I'm determined to get this done.'

- 'Keep smiling.'

- 'I'm much tougher than people think.'

- 'Think of the benefits when you finish!'

- 'Stay confident.'

- 'I've done this before – I can do it again!'

Memorise your CATs or jot them on a sheet of card to keep at hand. Then repeat your CATs to yourself whenever you need a lift. Verbalise them out loud with strength and certainty. Or go over them silently in your head if you could be overheard.

Need convincing that CATs work? Psychologist Michael Mahoney, then at Pennsylvania State University, studied a group of gymnasts hoping to qualify for the US Olympic team. He asked the gymnasts to talk about their thoughts during competitions. He found that the most successful athletes – those who qualified for the Olympic team – had as many doubts and worries as the less successful ones. However, the successful athletes constantly encouraged themselves by engaging in more positive self-talk. Tell yourself that you can do it and you go a long way towards proving yourself right.

If they can do it ...

Nick is a 38-year-old human resources manager who has always considered his strength to be with people rather than numbers. However, he has been asked by his boss to perform some in-depth analyses of the organisation's employee absenteeism and retention data. He feels he can't turn the request down without damaging his career credibility. So, despite believing that he isn't very good with numbers, he has to give it a go.

To assist him on his way, he jots down several capability-affirming thoughts (CATs) to repeat back to himself as he slogs through the task. He picks the four that seem most appropriate to the task ahead:

- 'I can do it.'

- 'I can do anything I set my mind to.'

- 'I'm better than I give myself credit for.'

- 'Keep concentrating.'

Working on the task, he repeats the statements to himself – both silently in his head and quietly out loud if no one is in earshot. He finds that he is able to quell the anxiety he feels about having to work on the analytical problem. Plus he makes progress on it more quickly than he expected. He comes out of it feeling that he can handle whatever his job can throw at him – even those dreaded numbers.

I use CATs when I'm sat at my computer and feeling overloaded with work, with reports to write, invoices to send to clients, and more paperwork than I feel I can cope with. To ensure you get the best effect, choose CATs that are meaningful to you and your situation. What you say to yourself when you want to be a gracious guest at a cocktail party may differ from what you tell yourself when you're grappling with a tough problem at work.

Over to you

Can you think of a situation that's coming up in which you'd like to feel more confident? It could be at work or outside of it, in a situation where you're on your own or surrounded by people. What helpful CAT statements could you repeat to yourself? Write them down here.

- ....
- ....
- ....
- ....

Vanquishing your mental monsters

The CAT Confidence Booster is a great way to start rooting out your ANTs. But if the CAT is like a pistol for picking off ANTs, this next Confidence Booster is the big gun, your mega-missile, for blowing those ANTs away entirely.

Sometimes you may feel so emotionally overwrought, your thoughts and feelings so tightly intertwined, that it's difficult to think clearly at all. Perhaps you're worrying about an important speech you need to give. Maybe you're fretting about attending a big reunion party where lots of your old school or university friends might judge you. Or maybe you're lying in bed unable to sleep because you've got that big exam or test the next morning.

We are capable of feeling bad in so very many ways: angry, fearful, anxious, worried, hopeless, slightly sad or downright depressed, resentful, guilty, or ashamed. But you don't have to feel bad ever again.

The FACADe technique is a powerful tool for tackling worries by distinguishing between fact and fiction, separating out what you feel from what's actually going on. Thousands of research studies involving many tens of thousands of people have proven that you can shift the way you think. Use it and you will grow your confidence.

Confidence Booster: Giving form to your thoughts

When you're stuck in the emotional dumps, sit down with a notebook and work through the five steps of the FACADe technique.

1 **Feelings**. Begin by writing down the emotions you're experiencing such as anger, despair, anxiety, envy, shame, embarrassment, and so on. Give each feeling a score from 0 to 10, depending on how strong each feeling is.

2 **Actions**. Write down how your behaviour has changed as a result of your feelings. What is it that your feelings are stopping you from doing? Or what is it that your emotions are pushing you to do? You might, for example, want to withdraw from a situation or avoid someone. Perhaps you want to shout and scream at someone. Or sit alone crying, drink yourself into oblivion, or any other number of unproductive actions.

3 **Circumstances**. Next, describe the circumstances, the situation, that has triggered your feelings. It could be something that happened in the past, is happening right now, or you're anticipating could happen

in the future. It could be an event, how someone has been behaving, or even an image or memory in your mind. Whatever is making you feel upset, write it down.

4 **ANTs**. Write down the thoughts or beliefs that are popping into your head. Look out for all of those negative thoughts about yourself, those criticisms, and unhelpful comments such as 'I'm hopeless' or 'They must think that I'm a real idiot'.

5 **Defects**. Finally, look for the defects, the flaws in your thoughts. Take each of your ANTs and rate how far you actually believe each one on a scale of 0 to 10. Look for ways to challenge each ANT. Imagine what you'd say to a friend who had that thought. What's a more constructive and compassionate thought that you could replace it with instead?

The FACADe technique takes a bit of getting used to but is the most robust tool we psychologists have for obliterating those pesky negative thoughts. But make sure you *write down* your answers to the five FACADe categories – don't just ponder them. Do it and you can separate your thoughts and emotions to find your more confident self again.

If they can do it ...

Kate has been on a diet and exercise programme for the last 3 weeks because she wants to get in shape for the office Christmas party. Not only that, but she will hit the big 50 next year so it feels a great time to restore her confidence in herself and her body. She bought a slinky black dress a couple of weeks ago and would love to fit into it in only 5 weeks' time. She was making good progress but went out on Friday night with 'the girls' for a quick drink that ended up turning into quite a lot of drinks followed by a midnight burger, fries, and extra mayonnaise on the side!

She feels desperately unhappy – totally gutted that she's blown her good efforts and ruined her diet. She doesn't know if she can be bothered to make a healthy meal today or go to the gym again. What's the point? But she decides to give the FACADe technique a shot.

Here's what she writes down as she works through the five steps.

1 **Feelings**. I feel truly guilty that I let myself down (6). But I also feel ashamed (8) because I've been telling people at work for the last few weeks how much progress I've made and now they think I'm a useless pig for stuffing myself on Friday night. I'm disappointed (5) in myself too.

2 **Actions**. Well, I've been sat on the sofa all morning because I don't know if I can be bothered to go to the supermarket to trawl the aisles for healthy food. I could make a quick call and have a 14-inch pizza delivered right now that wouldn't take any effort at all. And I'm not sure if I want to go to the gym either. It's going to take another two or three gym sessions to burn off all the food I wolfed down last night.

3 **Circumstances**. It was all last night. I knew that I shouldn't have had that first drink. I knew that 'only one' would turn into two, three, and then more. And I should have known better – I always fancy a burger when I've had a few to drink!

4 **ANTs**. Okay, here goes. I'm thinking:

   ▩ My friends at work think I'm a fat pig.

   ▩ I'm a useless fat pig.

   ▩ I'm never going to get into that new dress for the party.

5 **Defects**. Dr Rob's book says to look for the flaws in each ANT, so I'll take each one in turn.

Do my friends really think I'm a fat pig? No. I know Jane has tried to lose weight loads of times too so she's hardly going to laugh at me when I've been so supportive of her. And the rest of the girls really are my friends too. I'd never laugh at them if they had a rough day, so they're probably not thinking I'm a fat pig either. In any case, I know better than to try to read their minds. I'm not psychic!

I am a pig. But then again I'm not supposed to label myself. So maybe I should say that I pigged out on this occasion rather that I'm a pig! And I shouldn't say that I'm useless either. I need to tell myself that I let myself down on this occasion – but it's the only time I've slipped up in three weeks!

I'm probably being a bit overdramatic about never getting into that dress. I still have five weeks and if I go to the gym an extra time this week, I can make up for last night's blow out. Right, I need to get to the supermarket and buy those groceries so I can get to the gym before it closes this evening!

How about using the FACADe technique for yourself now? Think back to a situation that made you feel unhappy and challenge your thoughts and feelings.

Use it once, then again and again. Keep using the technique, don't let your guard down too quickly. Because ANTs are stubborn little buggers, just like an ant infestation in your garden. If you don't pay attention, they can sneak back in and wreak havoc all over again. They bury themselves deep underground and it takes time to eliminate them entirely.

But if you practise the FACADe, the longer your ANTs will stay away. With enough practice, you should be able to recognise your ANTs without writing them down. Eventually, spotting and challenging your ANTs could become a new habit, an instinct that's as natural as breathing or blinking.

You can sidestep the trap of negative thinking by cross-examining what's going on in your head. But you have to remember to use the technique when you're feeling glum or negative about yourself. I know people who write the word FACADe on sticky notes that they can post on their fridge, car dashboard, computer keyboard, and so on. How will you remember?

Taking your thoughts to task

Looking for defects in your thoughts, the fifth step of the FACADe technique, is perhaps the hardest. While you may easily name your emotions and recognise the thoughts that are running through your head, you may feel as if you don't have the right to challenge your thoughts.

To give yourself the best shot at catching the flaws in your ANTs, imagine that you're a third party – a sympathetic friend – interrogating your own beliefs. Ask yourself the following questions:

- Are you jumping to the worst possible conclusions? (For example, a friend doesn't turn up to meet you and you automatically assume that he hates you and doesn't want to see you again.) Remember that situations happen for all sorts of reasons and your automatic thought is unlikely to be the only explanation.

- Are you using words such as 'always' or 'never' to make overly sweeping statements about yourself based on a single event? (For example, being rejected after one job interview but thinking 'I'll *never* get a better job'.) Ask yourself whether your 'always' or 'never' statement is perhaps overdramatic based on just one or two incidents.

- Are you predicting a terrible future rather than waiting to see what happens? (For example, 'I'm going to fail that exam' or 'My boss is bound to turn down my request – so why bother asking?') No one can predict the future, so don't do it.

- Are you labelling yourself as a failure, worthless, or useless rather than as a person who has failed? (For example, thinking 'I'm such a *failure*' rather than 'I failed on that occasion but I can try again next time'.) Remind yourself that setbacks and mistakes do not make you a failure but merely someone who needs to try a different approach next time.

- Are you trying to read someone else's mind? (For example, automatically thinking 'He's yawning so he must think I'm really boring' rather than that he might be tired.) As you can't possibly read anyone else's mind, give other people the benefit of the doubt.

- Are you using words such as 'must', 'should', 'ought', or 'have to' to make excessive demands on yourself or other people? (For example, thinking 'I must not let people down' and then lambasting yourself because you had to let someone down.) If you find yourself falling into this trap, go on to ask yourself: why? Why *must* or *should* you or anyone else *have to* do anything? Try to be more flexible with yourself.

- Are you belittling your own achievements? (For example, thinking 'That was easy – anyone could have done it' or turning a friend's positive comment on its head to think 'He's only saying that because he feels sorry for me – I'm such a loser'.) It's a tough world out there already; you don't need to rubbish your own triumphs.

Ask yourself questions and you poke holes in the unhelpful beliefs you hold. Do it often enough and you will soon feel more positive and confident about yourself and the world around you.

Looking on the bright side

Modern life is full of ambiguous meanings. From vaguely phrased emails to half-heard conversations, it's easy to jump to the wrong conclusions about other people's intentions. A friend who hasn't returned your calls might be busy rather than upset with you.

Almost any situation can be interpreted in any number of ways. Remember that your beliefs are not the same as reality. Your beliefs are just one way of thinking about a situation or set of circumstances. Beliefs are rarely 'right' or 'wrong', but they can be empowering or disempowering, constructive or destructive. So why not choose to replace a disempowering belief with a more enabling one? Believe the best about yourself and you may surprise yourself by achieving it.

The FACADe technique for challenging the nasty ANTs that scuttle into your mind is a powerful weapon in your arsenal for protecting your self-confidence. But once you've challenged and eliminated your unhelpful beliefs, you can further grow your confidence by replacing them with more positive ones.

Earlier in this chapter I suggested that six people who got rejected after a job interview could interpret it in different ways, with the result that a few felt good and most felt bad. But if six people can think about the same situation in six different ways, then one person can think about a single situation in six different ways too. The friend who hasn't returned your calls could be snowed under with work or wrestling with a personal crisis. She could have lost your number or had her mobile stolen. Maybe she is waiting until the right opportunity so that you can meet in person rather than talk on the telephone. And because you can't know for certain what is going on with her, you do yourself no favours by clinging on to the worst possible explanation.

This next Confidence Booster is about generating alternative explanations.

Confidence Booster: Pondering possibilities

Once you've listed and smashed the negative thoughts that may be dragging you down, you can replace them with more constructive thoughts that will lift your confidence.

Write out the first ANT that has been bugging you. Then write down a handful of alternative interpretations that could replace it. If you're feeling down, you may have to work hard to think of other ways of looking at the situation, but persevere with it. Hold a mini-brainstorm and write down anything that comes to mind for now. Imagine other possible explanations for the situation you're in.

- What are other possible ways of looking at the situation?

- Have you any past experiences that could suggest an alternative perspective on what's happening?

- Would you encourage a friend to think this way?

- What would you say to a friend who was feeling down about the same situation?

Think creatively and aim to come up with at least a handful of alternatives. Six is a good number, but three will do. Then choose a constructive and realistic alternative belief. Draw a big circle around your chosen new thought. Write it in big letters on a separate piece of paper; say it out loud with conviction, as if you already believe it. Developing even one realistic explanation to replace an ANT is often enough to enable you to feel better.

You may be wondering whether it's realistic to replace a negative thought with a positive one. But I'm not asking you to replace your ANT with *any* positive thought that occurs to you.

I'm not suggesting you should ignore the facts and pretend that the world is a fantastic place – that would be naïve and phoney. You have to choose an alternative thought that is feasible and realistic given the evidence of the situation. But if you can find a good enough alternative explanation, you may find your confidence showing up again.

If they can do it ...

Ben, 24, works as an account manager for a computer supplies company. He had a sales meeting in which he was trying to persuade the client to buy one of his company's products. When the client turned him down, he felt really low. He blamed himself. But rather than let it crush his confidence, he used the FACADe technique to identify his ANTs. He found that his biggest and most persistent ANT was: 'I'm no good at selling.' To break free of his ANT, Ben writes down as many plausible explanations as he can think of:

- 'The client is a grumpy person and turns nearly everybody down.'

- 'I did a decent job but the client doesn't feel the timing is right to buy one of our products.'

- 'The client is having a bad day at work and I was unlucky enough to have met him today.'

- 'My company's products simply aren't right for the client; none of my colleagues could have persuaded the client to buy.'

- 'The client is a moron and couldn't grasp what I was getting at.'

- 'The client is preoccupied with problems in his personal life and isn't positively predisposed to *anyone* at the moment.'

The simple act of writing down a half-dozen explanations helps Ben to keep matters in perspective. He chooses to adopt 'I did a decent job but the client doesn't feel the timing is right to buy one of our products' as his new belief. He says it out loud a few times and finds that his mood begins to lift fairly quickly.

Nurturing a positive outlook

I'm going to toss a coin and make you an offer. Heads I give you £100 (or Yen, Dollars, Euros, whatever you like). Tails you give me £100 (or Yen, Dollars, or Euros). Can I tempt you to take the bet? Probably not, because the odds aren't that great.

But what if heads I give you £100 but tails you give me just £90 – would you take that bet now? Tempting, but still maybe not. We could go on, reducing the amount you'd have to lose until you were willing to take the bet.

Psychologist and Nobel prize winner Daniel Kahneman at Princeton University has found that most people would need to be offered a gain that's twice as large as the loss. So I'd put up £100 whereas you'd risk only £50.

The implication? The human mind is naturally attuned to feel loss more acutely than gain, to focus on negatives over positives, to agonise over risk rather than relish opportunity. But your outlook on life is not fixed. Science shows that you can change it.

I'm talking about optimism here. Optimists tend to look for what is good in the world, give themselves credit for their achievements, and focus on the pursuit of success. Pessimists, on the other hand, look for what is wrong in the world, attribute their achievements to dumb luck, and focus on the avoidance of failure. Which would you rather be – an optimist or pessimist?

Some people feel that having a negative outlook on life protects them. By expecting the worst, they can't be disappointed. But negativity doesn't protect you – it isolates you. If you don't believe me, try this little experiment: make yourself act in an optimistic and happy fashion with one person, and then negative and sad with another person. I'm sure you can appreciate that your attitude and outlook can affect how other people perceive you and treat you in turn. Pessimism breeds more negativity and closes doors. Optimism draws people to you and opens up opportunities you might otherwise ignore.

CONFIDENCE

Over to you

Ask yourself:

- Do you have a more positive or negative outlook on life?

- What do you believe are the benefits of having your outlook on life?

- Being honest with yourself, what do you think are the disadvantages of having your particular outlook?

Now you might think that your outlook on the world is something you are born with. But that's not right. Research has shown that whatever your current view of life, you can hone your level of optimism; you get more of what you focus on. So let's look at what's going well in your life every day.

Confidence Booster: Developing your sense of optimism

You can pass light through a prism to refract and separate out the colours of the rainbow. In a similar fashion, you can pass your experience through a more positive lens to focus on the more affirming highlights of your life.

Each evening, simply write down three things for which you feel grateful. These could be events that happened during the day, attributes you possess, relationships you have, or other good things you enjoy. Choose to interpret 'things for which you feel grateful' in whatever way you wish – I don't want to give you examples because you need to find what is noteworthy to you. You may choose to savour whatever pleasurable, enjoyable, or meaningful experiences you wish, no matter how great or small. If this was your last day on Earth, you'd probably find lots to appreciate. Write as much or as little about each one as you feel comfortable with. Although do describe not only *what* happened but also *why* it happened – in other words, how you made it happen.

I know the 'good things' technique sounds too simple, too good to be true. But there's hard science behind it. Professor Martin Seligman is one of the most respected psychologists in the world today. He and his crack team of researchers at the University of Pennsylvania compared the benefits of different techniques and found that this is the most powerful of the many they tested. Many other self-help techniques enhance confidence for a few weeks or a month. But even using this technique for just one week produces confidence-boosting effects up to six months later.

By looking out for a mere three good things a day, you train yourself to appreciate what is going well in your life. You begin to notice many more positive events, interactions, and moments. You achieve sustainable increases in your mood and confidence.

Seeing success

If you get nervous pangs before a social event, speech, or interview, you may visualise terrible scenarios such as spilling a drink, blushing, or other social *faux pas*. But if you can visualise bad things happening, you can visualise good things too.

Another way to build stronger beliefs is to exploit the power of positive visualisation. If you've ever been bored and let your mind drift into a bit of a daydream – I know I have plenty of times! – you can harness the gift of visualisation.

Sports people have used visualisation for decades as a tool to enhance their performance. By picturing what they want to happen – being the first to cross the finish line, making the perfect golf swing, landing a triple Axel – they make it more likely to happen.

Hard science confirms the power of visualisation too. Stephen

Kosslyn, a professor of psychology at Harvard University, used brain-scanning equipment to show that imagining a movement activates the same parts of the brain that light up during the actual movement. Specialised cells in the brain called mirror neurons are activated simply by *thinking* about an activity. From the brain's point of view, imagining an activity is very similar to executing it.

In case you're still not convinced, I'll share with you another recent piece of research. Professor Leslie Walker is a UK-based researcher looking at the effects of positive visualisation on cancer. Astonishingly, Professor Walker says that patients who can picture the treatment battling the cancer or visualise their tumours disappearing, achieve better outcomes. Think about that for a moment: visualisation can affect the progress of one of the most feared diseases in the modern world. So, how relatively easy should it be for you to use visualisation to fuel your confidence?

Run through an event in your head and you help yourself to perform at your confident best. Take that driving test, speak at a seminar, play the violin solo at a concert. Do it in your mind and prep yourself for the real thing.

Get ready to succeed

Some people have a mental block and think they can't visualise. But anyone can do it and here's a tiny example. I want you to imagine you're on your way home. You've had a long day and now you're standing in front of the door to your house. What do you see? What colour is the door? Where's the keyhole and what does it look like? Is there a letterbox, a handle or a doorknob? There you go, you can do it. Visualisation is nothing more than picturing images in your head. You *can* do it.

Confidence Booster: Using the movie screen in your head

Visualisation is like sitting back and watching the movie of the book of your life. Imagine you have been so successful in your life that someone has written a book about you. Not only that, but a movie studio has turned your book into a film. And now you're watching a segment of that film, the bit where you overcome your fears to deliver a sterling performance.

Find a quiet place for your visualisation. Get away from ringing telephones, noisy colleagues, rumbling trains, screaming kids, and give it a go.

▨ Think about the upcoming event or situation you want to feel more confident about. Perhaps it's asking your boss for a pay rise, making sparkling conversation at a party. Giving the toast at a wedding, serving a bunch of aces in a tennis tournament, or having a tough conversation with a loved one. Imagine the scene as if you were watching it on a movie screen.

▨ Begin by fleshing out how you look and what you're wearing. You'd be calm and composed, maybe smiling slightly, perhaps laughing a lot. What about your clothes? A smart suit, a sexy outfit, tennis whites and training shoes. Add the detail to how you look.

▨ Run the scene as you would *like* it to happen. *Imagine yourself enjoying the experience.* Envision yourself negotiating confidently with your boss, delighting your dinner date, getting rapturous applause from your audience. Remember that this is how you *want* the event or situation to go – so allow yourself to be a superstar in your mental movie.

▨ Play the scene back and add detail to make the mental images as vivid as possible. Add colour and depth and textures to make it breathtakingly real.

▨ Involve your other senses in the mental movie too. I know it's called visualisation, but now we're turning your movie into a 3D immersive experience. Hear the words you want to say and the sounds around you – the congratulations of your boss or the laughter of your fellow partygoers. Smell the leather of the interviewer's armchair. Taste the creamy cheesecake you're sharing with your loved one. Feel the weight and coldness of the trophy as you lift it over your head.

▨ Finally, add your emotions too. How does the scene make you *feel*? It goes without saying we're talking about positive emotions here. But do you want to feel calm and focused or excited and animated?

You need to run through your mental movie a couple of times to lock it into your mind. But that's all there is to visualisation. It's more straightforward to see your success than you might imagine.

Visualisation can allow all of us to enhance our readiness for that Big Event, the one you're feeling a little tense or downright anxious about. As with many of the techniques in this book, you need to practise to get better. Practising it will enable you to summon up those mental movies more easily and more vividly each time. The more effort you put into visualising a successful outcome, depicting with crystal clarity what you want to happen, the more your feelings of confidence will increase. How about you attempt it right now?

ONWARDS AND UPWARDS

▨ Remember that your beliefs are merely your personal interpretation of what is happening to you – your beliefs are not the same as reality. If you have negative beliefs, you feel bad about yourself and the world. If you have positive beliefs, you feel strong and confident.

▨ Your inner critic judges you more harshly than anyone else ever could. Take heart that, when you feel self-conscious, you are probably being judged by the voice in your head rather than the people around you.

■ You are not born with your beliefs. Yes, your thoughts may pop automatically into your head. But you can make a conscious effort to challenge them and shed unhelpful notions about yourself.

■ Choose to adopt a more optimistic view of life. This isn't about putting on rose-tinted spectacles and pretending that the world is a wonderful place, but simply choosing to focus on what is good in your life rather than dwelling only on what is bad.

■ Use the potent – yet often overlooked – technique of visualisation for overcoming worries and preparing to tackle challenging situations.

■ But if you need to maintain your confidence when you're in the middle of a sticky situation, use the CAT (capability-affirming thought) technique to replace negative thoughts with more positive ones.

■ Your beliefs have built up over many years. So bear in mind that it may take repeated attempts to combat the effects of your unhelpful beliefs and replace them with more positive ones.

03

Setting confident goals

"If one advances confidently in the direction of his dreams,
and endeavours to live the life which he has imagined, he
will meet with a success unexpected in common hours."
Henry David Thoreau, author

In this chapter you will...

▨ create a picture of a confident future to motivate you into action

▨ uncover the personal values that will allow you to live a contented and confident life

▨ set effective goals that you will actually want to achieve

▨ take practical steps to creating the more confident you

▨ learn techniques to overcome laziness and procrastination.

The Spice Girls are the biggest-selling all-female pop group in history. Their debut single *Wannabe* sold millions worldwide despite some ropey lyrics. I'm sure you know the song – the one that tells you 'what I want, what I really really want'. And then you find out that what they 'really really really' want is a 'zigazig ha'.

Excuse me? I'm not even sure if 'zigazig ha' is a verb or a noun, an action or a thing. But whatever it is, the Spice Girls really, really want it. So what do *you* really, really want?

There's a saying that you can do *anything*, but you can't do *everything*. If you don't set goals, you end up aimless, adrift, perpetually scattering your energy in 20 directions and going nowhere. With goals, you can set a clear direction, make plans, and take action.

If you're like most people, you've made New Year's resolutions in the past. Maybe to get in better shape, get a new job, be more sociable, quit a bad habit, save more money – you know the kind of thing. But, still assuming you're like most people, you've failed to keep them too. We're all busy and other stuff ends up getting in the way; so we lapse back into old, bad habits.

The good news is that a solid foundation of research and

practice shows how to set effective goals that you will be looking forward to achieving. And so I'm going to share these tips with you to help you get what you really, really want.

Peering into the crystal ball

Wouldn't it be great to be able to see the future? To know the next set of lottery numbers, what's going to happen to house prices, and how your job, relationship, health, children, and everything else will turn out. Of course no one can. But you can do the next best thing: you can *create* your own future.

Confident people do not merely wait for the future to unfold – they make the future happen. If they want the top job and the corner office, they figure out what they must achieve to get it. If they want to settle down and start a family, they create the opportunities to meet a prospective partner. And that's what you're going to do too. You are going to take control of your life by creating a vision of the life you want.

'Vision?' I hear you ask. A vision is simply a picture of where you would like your life to go. If life is a journey, what's *your* destination? When you know you are heading for a worthwhile future, you start to see the predicaments and obstacles you encounter as mere inconveniences on the way to achieving your future. You feel in control and confident because you know that your actions are moving you towards your vision.

Most confident people have a vision of where they want to go – not a rigid plan but at least a broad direction. They may not call them visions, but that doesn't mean that they don't have them. They may think of them as long-term goals, plans, or ambitions. Or their sense of purpose and meaning in life. But the point is that they have them.

Get ready to succeed

Start to collect a mental dossier of people you admire – perhaps friends, colleagues, people in the public eye, or even people from history or fiction that you've read about. Consider what it is about each of them you admire. Ask yourself: what does that tell you about what you want in your own life?

A vision inspires you to make plans and take action. Having a vision is like booking a holiday. When it comes to choosing a holiday destination, you have so many choices. You could ski in Aspen, walk in the Lake District, shop in New York, sightsee in Beijing, trek in India, sun-worship in the Bahamas. But you can't plan or get excited about it until you make a decision and know where you're going. Only when you can see yourself sipping a cocktail on the beach or feeling the crunch of fresh snow under your boots can you get *really* fired up. Only then can you make plans about what to pack, how to get there, what jabs you might need, what you want to do, where you want to visit. And in the meantime if you have a bad day, you only need bring to mind your impending holiday to make you feel warm and cheery inside.

And that's what your vision can do for you. Your vision is there to:

■ excite you and inspire you to make plans

■ remind you of the brilliant future that could be yours

■ keep you motivated and working towards it until you achieve it.

The human being is the only animal that can think about the future, so you may as well use that talent. Whether your long-term aspirations are to be confident and popular in your social life or a successful business person, a winning sports player or a great parent, you need a vision to get you there.

Over to you

Vision is big stuff, but you can start off smaller. I call this one the Tombstone Test.

- In 10 words or less, write down: what motto would you like inscribed on your tombstone?

- What does your chosen phrase say about what you would like to achieve and be remembered for in your life?

"As long as you are going to think anyway – you might as well think big!"

Donald Trump, entrepreneur

Take Action: Creating your vision

Your vision should be an inspirational picture of your future – how you would *like* your life to turn out rather than how it is *likely* to turn out. Because your vision should include everything you want to achieve in life, it should feel at least a little scary, but hopefully also be awe-inspiring. Get it right and your vision should put a big smile on your face every time you think about it.

Come on, this is your chance. Your future can be better than your past or present. Dream big. If your life could go as well as it possibly could, what would it look like?

Make sure you're in a positive and upbeat mood before you start this exercise. Perhaps engage in a favourite activity beforehand so you feel calm and optimistic.

Then find a time and place where you can enjoy a half-hour or so of uninterrupted thought. Envisage a special birthday party thrown in your honour, say five or ten years in the future. See in your mind's eye a momentous occasion with all of the key people in your life there to celebrate with you. This is a special gathering because it marks a decade since you decided to change your life. You have worked hard, overcome hurdles, and achieved the goals you set yourself. Now hear the joy and laughter in the air. See the glasses raised to toast the person that you are, the life that you have lived, and the successes you have achieved. You have asked a handful of the most important people in your life to give speeches in your honour. What would they say about you?

Formulate your own vision by working through the following steps:

1 Let your imagination go a little wild. Avoid merely extrapolating your current life into the future. Your vision should capture a sense of what is *possible*, not what is *probable*. Imagine that the next 10 years have gone well. How would that future look and feel?

2 Think about the handful of key people you would like to be giving speeches about you. Choose people who would be able to speak about the different areas of your fantastic life.

3 Write down in detail what you would like each of them to say about you. Think about the seven spheres of a confident life: your physical health, intimate relationships, family and social life, career, money, and purpose in life. Remember also your strengths from the exercises in Chapter 1. Each speech should aim to capture not only your achievements but also the strengths you used to get where you are.

4 Consider your response to all of the speeches. As the guest of honour, you can't get away without sharing your thoughts about your journey over the last decade. What would you say? What are the highlights you want to comment on? How did you use your strengths to get where you are? And how does it *feel* to be where you are now?

If they can do it ...

Alex, 28, has been working as an assistant manager for a high street retailer for four years. He has a comfortable life, renting a room from a married couple, and he has a solid group of friends. However, he feels both bored and frustrated with his work, with being single, with not having enough money to get his own place. And he realises that if he doesn't do something, he could easily become a 38-year-old assistant manager living the same life, renting a room, feeling the same way.

But no longer. He decides to take control. He writes out how he would like his future to turn out.

It's my fortieth birthday party and my friends, family and girlfriend are gathered with me to celebrate. And it's a double celebration as the boss of the technology consultancy that I work for last week asked me to become a partner in the firm.

My dad is the first to stand and speak: 'Happy birthday son. I am so proud of you. When you were in your late 20s, I felt that you were drifting and that you could have easily coasted into your 30s and 40s and the rest of your life without achieving anything of note.

'Of course I'm proud of your career achievements. Going back to college to take that software engineering course was the beginning of turning your life around. But what I'm most proud of is that you've made such an effort with your family. You seem to have spent your 20s pulling away from the rest of us, but now you're a fantastic uncle to your nephews and nieces. And you still come home to visit your dear old parents! Happy birthday again and I hope that it won't be long before you are tying the knot with your better half too.'

Next to toast my success is my close friend Peter: 'Happy birthday you old dog. I really didn't think you'd amount to anything. I thought you were going to be the same old Alex forever, always needing to borrow a few pounds until the end of the month, which I knew I'd never get back. But here we are celebrating in this magnificent house. Your kitchen is bigger than my entire flat!

'But the combination of your studying and hard work has paid off and you deserve everything that you've got now. Well done and enjoy your day!'

Finally, my boss and friend (I'm going to call him William) finishes off the toasts: 'I hired you because you struck me as a young man who was determined to succeed. Yes, you had your critics who said that you hardly had any experience. But you impressed us with the ferocious determination in your eyes. You told me that if I hired you, you'd work whatever hours it took to get the job done. And you've been as good as your word. So I am proud and very pleased to be able to celebrate both your birthday and the fact that you will as of January be a full partner in the firm. Congratulations!'

Over to you

Even if you don't have a half-hour right now to write out your vision, you can certainly spend a few minutes daydreaming. Allow yourself to wonder about your ideal future life. Go on, do it now. Close your eyes or gaze out of the window and let your mind's eye fast forward into the future:

■ What are you doing?

■ Who are you with?

■ What's going on at work and outside of it?

Let your imagination off its leash. Just make sure you're not operating heavy machinery while you're doing it!

What's the *worst* thing that could happen if you pursue your vision? Well, you may not achieve it; you may end up where you are now. But what's the *best* thing that could happen if you pursue your vision? Imagine if you achieved it *all* . . .

Picture perfect

Here's an alternative idea for you. Your vision is a picture of the future, so why not draw it if you like? You may have heard that most people favour either the left- or right-side of their brain. Left-brainers think in a logical, linear fashion and typically prefer writing to drawing. Right-brainers are more creative and more switched on by images than words.

I'm a left-brainer. I feel strong writing my thoughts down and uncomfortable when drawing or being the slightest bit creative. But I know right-brainers who love images and feel stifled by words. If you want to create your vision in a form other than words, do it. Cut out pictures from magazines to fill a scrap book or create a collage. Draw a representation of your vision or turn it into a comic strip. Create a papier maché sculpture of it or shoot a video diary of yourself. Do what works for you. Just make sure you do it.

Living an authentic life

Remember this is your vision, your life. Your vision should capture your authentic aims and ambitions and not those of your friends or colleagues, parents or siblings, neighbours or anyone else. Many people find themselves being influenced by what they think they *should* or *ought* to do. But someone else's bliss could be your personal drudgery.

Don't settle for what you have just because everyone else seems to be doing it. Don't get a mortgage and put down roots because you're expected to. So what if everyone else is chasing a bigger salary and flashy job title if that's not what you want? Enough!

You have to say the hell with everyone else's expectations and decide to live your life how you want. Go for what *you* want rather than what seems socially acceptable. True confidence comes from pursuing your own dreams and not those of the people around you.

"I don't know the key to success, but the key to failure is to try to please everyone."

Bill Cosby, comedian

Vision or daydream?

The difference between a vision and a daydream

Vision	Daydream
Depends on your efforts	Depends on luck (e.g. 'I wish I could win the lottery' or 'I wish a talent scout would discover me')
Puts you in control	Allows others to take control
Encourages you to take responsibility for making things right	Allows you to blame other people or circumstances for things being wrong
Creates the right circumstances	Waits for circumstances to be right
Inspires you to create a plan of action	Enters your thoughts occasionally but never for long
Is achieved through a little effort every day	Is realised in an unlikely flash or instant
Requires action today	Puts action off for another day

A vision is a motivating picture of what you hope to *achieve* because achieving distinguishes a vision from a mere daydream. A daydream is just an idle thought with no actions, no results, while a vision inspires you to take action.

Wish upon a star or treat yourself like one. The choice is yours. If you only *wish* you could change, shrug your shoulders and do nothing, then the only person you let down is yourself. Take charge. Put this book down right now and *do* something. Even if it's only to reach for a pen to capture your ideas on paper, take action!

Leading a life worth living

"This above all: To thine own self be true."

William Shakespeare, playwright

What do you value? What's important to you? If you could only be or have one thing, what would it be? It's a big question – real 'meaning of life' stuff. In fact, it *is* about the meaning of life: what's the meaning of *your* life?

Values are a set of standards or guidelines, a code of conduct, for how people live their lives. People who are spiritual might call it their morals or mores. Others might call it their attitude to or philosophy of life. But what you call it is less important than what it allows you to do. Your values are what matters to you, what you care about and hold dear. People who live according to their values are fulfilled and contented. People who have to compromise on their values feel frustrated if not downright depressed.

Now you may think that sounds a bit grand. That you don't live your life by any rules or principles. If you're like most people, you probably don't spend a lot of time thinking about your values. But that doesn't mean you don't have them.

Say you work for a boss who treats people like dirt because the only thing that matters to him is making money. If that rubs you the wrong way, perhaps your values are more to do with people – or at least not so much about making money at all costs. Or a friend of yours is always forgetting to return your calls. If that annoys you to your core, then you probably have a value that is something to do with keeping your promises or being loyal to friends. When you approve or disapprove of the actions and circumstances of the people around you, that's often a good indicator as to what your values may be.

Confident, successful people have a vision *and* know their values – and so should you. Your vision mostly depicts what you would like to achieve. But your values define what you are and aren't willing to do, how you will and won't behave, to achieve it.

You may not currently be living your life according to your values. Life isn't always easy and people have to make compromises to get themselves through the day. But once you've identified your values and begin to live by them, you will experience a new sense of freedom. You can let go of stuff that isn't important to you and instead focus only on what matters.

Over to you

Your values may be more important to you than you realise. Identify a time when your values were put to the test. Consider the following:

- What was the situation?
- What did you do or how did you feel?
- What did you learn about yourself and your values?

Take Action: Uncovering your values

The following is a list of possible values. Some are tangible values, including wealth and possessions. A few describe situations or circumstances such as security and geographical location. Others are personal characteristics such as integrity and kindness. Which ones stand out as being of the greatest importance to you? Start by circling however many you like or copying them out on to a fresh sheet of paper.

Friends	Influence	Accomplishment	Personal growth
Challenge	Contribution to society	Creativity	Respect
Predictability	Family	Integrity	Excitement
Excellence	Status	Kindness	Autonomy
Authority	Solitude	Helping others	Fun
Loving partner	Humour	Stability	Loyalty
Being needed	Personal possessions	Peace	Being attractive
Learning	Health	Responsibility	Security
Freedom	Adventure	Spiritual growth	Success
Control	Making a difference	Routine	Sporting ability
Your faith	Honesty	Equity ownership	Location
Recognition	The environment	Being wanted	Children
Independence	Affiliation	Love	Community
Power	Travel	Art/aesthetics	Wealth

No list of values could ever be comprehensive. Add whatever other words or phrases you feel could better capture what you value. Think about people you work or socialise with as well as people you've read or heard about. What do you like about how they live their lives? What do they do that you wish you could do too?

You may feel that many of these values play a part in your life. To be useful though, you need to identify your *core* values. Your values should help you to weigh up alternatives and make better choices. If a choice takes you away from or against one of your values, you know immediately to find another route to take. But if you have too many values, you can't make effective decisions. Practically speaking, a list of more than 10 or so values is little better than having none at all. Ten values should be your maximum but fewer are even better.

Think about what each value means to you. Is it an integral part of your life or merely a nice-to-have? How would you feel if it were taken away from you?

Next, turn each of your core values into a guideline that you can follow, live your life by, and make decisions with. How do you see that value steering your behaviour? For example, three different people who each include 'family' in their set of values could create different rules as follows:

■ 'I put my family first in *everything* I do. Even if my career prospects suffer as a result, but so long as I earn enough money to put a roof over their heads and food on the table, my family knows that they always come first.'

■ 'I spend every Saturday with my family. That doesn't mean that I need to give up what I love (like going to home rugby matches). But if I'm to do the things I love, I have to persuade – not force – my family to be a part of my activities too.'

■ 'I put my family at the heart of everything I do, but I'm not going to be unrealistic about it. I aim to spend at least three evenings a week getting home from work early enough to eat with them, read to the children, and put them to bed. If I can't do that occasionally, I'm not going to punish myself over it.'

Your final step is to rank your values statements. You could write your shortlist of values on sticky notes and shuffle the list around until you have your most deeply cherished value at the top. Or simply rewrite your list, numbering them in order of priority.

Avoid, if you can, having tied rankings in your list of values. Life often involves trade-offs. We only have 24 hours in the day and you can't be in two places at once. If you want to be rich, you may have to say no to social and personal relationships more times than you would like. If you crave excitement and adventure in your life, you may not be able to make as much money as your peers. If you want to be remembered above all for your kindness, you may have to sacrifice honesty and go along with the occasional white lie.

I'm not suggesting that you concoct a list of prescriptive rules and live your life in a regimented or inflexible way. Your values are a set of guidelines – not regulations – and it's up to you to interpret them in different situations. But by identifying your deep-seated values, you can weigh up options and opportunities to see which ones sit best with your principles. You can allocate time and energy to tasks and situations that matter to you and remove yourself from ones that don't. People in history have died for their values; you can at least learn to make better choices and occasionally say no to people because of yours.

If they can do it ...

Nina, 41, works as a recruitment consultant. She is financially successful but recently has found herself getting irritable with colleagues and clients. Realising that her passions lie elsewhere, she wrote a vision and decided that she would love to run a restaurant. She recognises that this is a long-term goal that may take her a number of years, but in the meantime she uncovers her values to sustain her until she achieves her vision.

After selecting an initial list of over a dozen values, she pares them down to a final five. And here are the statements she writes to guide how she aims to live.

■ **Excitement**. 'I want a fresh challenge every day. I'd rather earn less but be entertained and surprised by what happens every day at work than be rich but bored.'

■ **Affiliation**. 'Having people around me that I like and trust is critical in all areas of my life. When I set up to do whatever I end up doing, I will do it in partnership with other people. I'd rather be part of a moderately successful and happy team than be massively successful on my own.'

■ **Husband**. 'Even though we've only been married a year, I realise that the "honeymoon period" will fade and that a marriage can require effort. I must never let my career get so busy that I neglect the relationship that I hope will sustain me for the rest of my life.'

■ **Health**. 'I can't be doing without eating healthily and exercising. Whatever my workload, I must ensure that I can swim a couple of times a week and look after myself.'

■ **Fairness**. 'Treating everyone I meet with respect and receiving respect from them is a must-have in my life. I've had to put up with some rubbish from clients in recent years, but no longer! If people aren't good for how I feel, I will find ways to remove them from my life.'

My last words on values are that it *almost* goes without saying that you have to be honest with yourself. Just as your vision needs to reflect your authentic desires in life, your values must stand for how *you* want to live – and not how you think you should be living. Given that no one else need ever see your list of values, the only person you'd deceive is yourself. So before we move on, look at your values statements and ask yourself:

■ Is every one of the values that you have chosen deeply important to you?

■ Are you sure that you're not creating a set of values that reflects what your parents or partner, friends, colleagues, or anyone else might deem appropriate?

- Do you feel good when you look at the list and feel that you've captured the person you would like to be?

If you answer 'no' to any of those questions, be careful that you're not trying to impose values on yourself that don't really reflect what would make you happy and confident. We all carry baggage with us from our upbringing, and the messages that we hear from society, organised religion, the media, and so on. So work on your values until you can look at them and feel happy that they represent the life you genuinely want to live.

"Above all be true to yourself, and if you cannot put your heart into it, take yourself out of it."

Hardy D. Jackson, author

A word of advice: Avoid the lure of the quick-fix

You may be thinking: vision and values?!? Maybe you picked up this book wanting to feel more confident in a couple of areas of your life, such as public speaking or dating, being a parent or socialising. And maybe now you've skipped the vision and values stuff and are heading straight to setting goals.

Of course that's your prerogative. Let's face it: most of us want a quick-fix. A miracle diet, an overnight relationship makeover, instant confidence. We like immediate, easy, painless results – and yes, you'll find other books or experts saying you can get confidence in a jiffy. But I'm sharing with you an approach that will give you the *best* confidence. You get out of this book what you put in.

The tools and techniques in this book work. They don't work without effort on your part. *But they work.* Decades of research by eminent scientists from around the world tell us the best ways to set goals and boost our confidence. Trust me – I'm a psychologist!

Tackling an isolated area or two of your life may seem like an attractive shortcut. But every aspect of your life is interconnected. Start working on a few areas of your life and you may discover there are opportunities to grow and develop in other areas of your life too. Only when you consider your life as a whole can you spot the best ways to invest your time and effort. And your path to your new, more confident whole life begins by considering your long-term vision and the values you hold dear.

So, can you spare the time to ponder your vision and values?

You can't be in the game without a goal

Great, you have your vision and values. You'll be pleased to hear that those are two of the hardest exercises to do in this book. If you've got those worked out, the rest should be a piece of cake!

Your vision is an exciting but broad picture of where you want to get to and what you want to achieve. You probably have some pretty big aspirations in your vision – you're selling yourself short if your vision isn't at least a little daunting. But how do you get there? Your values guide the big decisions in your life, but knowing that you want to live honestly and be successful, or to have fun with your family, doesn't tell you the steps you need to take to achieve your vision either. So how do you work out the steps you need to take?

To explain, let's consider that holiday you booked (back on page 58). Thinking about where you're going on holiday should make the excitement bubble up inside you. But to get ready for it, you need to make a list of tasks to complete. Get your holiday clothes out of storage and borrow a bigger suitcase from a friend. Drop off your favourite outfit at the dry cleaner. Dig out your passport. Buy a new pair of sunglasses and some Factor 15.

In the same way, you need to create specific goals and plans to achieve your vision. And until you achieve it, your vision motivates you to keep forging ahead, ticking the items off your goals and plans.

SPOT the goal

There's a lot of powerful psychology to setting effective goals. Study after study shows that people are more successful at following through on their goals when they consider exactly when and where and how they can work on them. All you need to do is remember the letters SPOT.

Stretching and significant

S is for stretching and significant. Okay, I cheated a little – there should be two 'S's. But your goal has to be both challenging and worthwhile.

Your goal has to be at least ambitious enough for you to need to push yourself to achieve it. Research shows that people often underestimate their ability. You're probably better than you think you are. So set yourself a goal that will stretch and challenge you. If you do that, you may surprise yourself as to what you can achieve.

But aim to stretch, not snap. Just as an elastic band has a point at which it stops stretching and simply snaps, you don't want to set yourself a goal that is so out-of-this-world that you couldn't possibly achieve it. A bit of stretch is more motivating than an easily attainable goal. But an unrealistic and entirely unattainable goal will only make you feel frustrated and fed up. So stretch, but don't snap.

The second 'S' refers to significance. Your goal has to be important, appealing, alluring. You have to want it. Badly. If your goal isn't exciting and a big deal, you could end up getting distracted. Sure, it would be nice to learn another language, but do you want to do it because you *should* or because you honestly love the idea and can't wait to fly off and try your new language skills? Yes, it would be cool to get that promotion, but is that because your other half is pressurising you or because you can't wait to take on more responsibility? Make sure you choose goals that make you want to jump up and down because *you* want them so much.

Positive

Imagine for a moment that you're on a diet and someone says to you: 'Don't eat any chocolate, don't think about the sound it makes as you break a piece off or the smell as you pop it into your mouth. And definitely don't think about the taste as it melts on your tongue and oozes down your throat.' What do you think you're going to end up thinking and obsessing about, craving and drooling over? Chocolate, of course.

When you set a goal, you get what you focus on. Set yourself a negative goal such as 'I want to worry less' and your mind focuses on the 'worry'. You end up worrying more. Tell yourself 'I don't want to embarrass myself in meetings' and your mind latches on to the word 'embarrass' – you end up feeling more self-conscious than before. Goals that contain 'don't' or 'not' or 'less' are self-defeating. Better then to set yourself positive goals such as 'I want to think more optimistically' or 'I want to be a confident participant in meetings'.

Research backs all of this up too. Laboratory studies show that people who set positive goals about what they want are more likely to achieve them than people who set negative goals about what they want to avoid.

You get the point. So how can you phrase your goals in terms of what you want to develop, gain, or hone?

Observable

Say you set yourself a goal to 'get better at socialising at parties'. How would you know when you've achieved it? Would talking to 20 new people get you the tick in the box? How about if you talk to only 10, 6 or 1 new person?

For a goal to be effective, it should be observable to other people whether you've reached it or not. Unless you quantify your goal, you won't know when to give yourself a pat on the back for achieving it. Your goal should be specific and obvious enough that an impartial onlooker could nod and say 'yes, you've achieved your goal' or, with a shake of the head, say 'no, not yet'.

Contrast these observable (and effective) versus opaque (and ineffective) goals:

Observable versus opaque goals

Observable goals	Opaque goals
'I will speak up at least three times during team meetings.'	'I want to get noticed during team meetings.'
'I want to get the name of my business mentioned in a national newspaper.'	'I want to be a famous entrepreneur.'
'I will be more adventurous by trying a small, new experience daily.'	'I want to be more adventurous with my choices in life.'
'I will call my parents once a week for at least a 10-minute chat.'	'I must make more of an effort with my parents.'

Timed

So you want to ask for that pay rise, overcome your fear of public speaking, find a hot date. Or stand up to someone, volunteer for charity work, set up your own business. The question is: when?

Deadlines are motivating. If you make a promise that you'll do something by a certain date, that's a much bigger commitment than saying 'you'll get round to it'. A deadline acts as a powerful reminder, a mental kick in the backside.

But set yourself too distant a deadline – 'I'll get that pay rise by the year 2025' – and you may as well not have one. On the other hand, aim to achieve it by next month and you may be putting yourself under too much time pressure. So choose a date for the completion of your goal that is challenging yet realistic. Choose a date that compels you to take action today, but not one that will drive you crazy with worry about how you're going to get it done in time.

Even better, if you can pick a significant deadline for it. Perhaps by your next birthday, wedding anniversary, Christmas, Hanukkah, date of the next England away-game, or anything else that will stick in your mind until you have achieved your goal.

You may be wondering: 'But what if I fail to achieve the goal by the allotted deadline? Wouldn't it be better to allow a bit of extra time to make doubly sure I can achieve my goal in time?' The answer's no. A big N-O. Sure, if you're delivering a project at work or promising to help a friend out by a certain date, you need to keep your promises. But when it comes to taking action in pursuit of your personal goals, a goal that compels you to take action sooner trumps a goal that allows you to take action later. Better to have achieved 80 to 90 per cent of your goal by the deadline than to have such a distant deadline that you can keep putting off action. Go on, give yourself a testing timeframe.

Here's the bit where you get involved

Okay, I've talked enough about setting effective goals. I'm sure you get the idea. SPOT – that's simple enough, right? But as I've mentioned before (and will mention again), you get the biggest benefits from this book by taking action and not just reading.

So what are your goals? How can you translate that broad picture of your amazing future into a set of concrete goals?

Take Action: What do you really, really want?

Your vision is an inspiring picture of the future you would like to achieve. Your values are a set of guidelines on how you should behave to feel strong and confident.

To translate your vision and values into a set of goals, consider: what are the three things you want most from your vision and values? Write these down by completing the sentence 'I want…' three times.

Of course, you may have more than three goals. But for now let's stick with three. When you're starting out on the path to a more confident life, you are better off having a small number of goals. If you have too many goals, you could end up spreading your efforts too thinly. When you've achieved or made significant progress on these initial three goals, you can always come back to your vision and add further new goals.

Next, take each of your three statements and rewrite it as a SPOT goal. Remember to make it Stretching and significant, Positive, Observable and Timed.

If they can do it …

Patrick is a 37-year-old successful graphic designer working in the
marketing department of an international healthcare company. He enjoys
the creative aspects of his job but works with large teams on enormous
projects, which means that he only gets to work on a tiny part of the
overall puzzle. He has been feeling for some time that he is a cog in a
huge machine and realises he needs to change something to avoid
feeling unfulfilled in his work for the rest of his life.

He completes the vision and values exercises and decides that he would
love to set up his own graphic design agency. His vision sees him at the
heart of a small business, with a few enthusiastic staff working for him.
And one of his core values is to have total control over his work. He
would be able to pursue smaller projects that he could work on in their
entirety rather than just fragments of larger ones.

To help him retain his focus, he turns his vision into a SPOT goal.

■ **Stretching and significant**. 'I want to set up my own business and
be able to choose the kinds of projects I do.' This goal feels pretty
stretching for him because he has never worked for himself; he needs
to learn about the administrative side of running a business. But it's
significant too as he really longs to work on smaller projects that he
can manage from beginning to end.

■ **Positive**. 'I want to earn enough money to pay my bills and allow me
to have at least two holidays a year.' He phrases his goal in terms of
what he wants rather than what he wants to avoid (e.g. 'I don't want
to have to worry about money').

■ **Observable**. 'I will start to look for new clients by researching small
companies that may need the services of a freelance graphic designer
– I will call 10 companies a day.' His goal is clearly observable as an
impartial onlooker could simply count the number of potential clients
that he calls every day.

■ **Timed**. 'I will be working for myself in six months' time.' Because he doesn't know everything he needs to know about running a business, he gives himself six months to research what he needs to do. By giving himself a deadline, he knows he will have to get a move on straightaway.

The power of the pen

You've got a vision, values and a set of goals now, right? If you haven't, please consider putting pen to paper or fingers on keyboard to capture the thoughts and dreams you have running around in your head. If you want to change your life and grow in confidence, then put your confidence in me. Trust me when I say you need to write up your vision, values, and goals before moving on.

Okay, if you don't believe me, trust the science. Back in the 1950s, a bunch of researchers asked Harvard University graduates about their goals. As you might expect, most of these fresh-faced kids had goals. But only 3 per cent of them actually wrote their goals down. Fast-forward 30 years to a follow-up survey and guess what? The 3 per cent had accumulated as much wealth as the other 97 per cent put together.

Now I know money doesn't buy happiness. But in my book it buys a nice house, a shiny car, and a few fun holidays, which make life that little bit more comfortable while you figure out what could be making you happy.

Writing stuff down has some kind of power. It makes your thoughts more real. You can't dismiss them as easily. You help yourself to succeed.

Baby steps for big results

Great, you've got a goal. And you've put them somewhere prominent to remind yourself of your commitments. What next?

I know it's a cliché to say that a journey of a thousand miles begins with a single step. But just because it has been said many times does not make it any less true.

Imagine that your goal is to run a marathon in a year's time. You'd have to be fairly daft to think that you could wake up on the morning of the race, put on your training shoes and run 26 miles. So how would you get ready for it? Of course, you'd start off by doing a short run. Or maybe a brisk walk if you're really out of shape. After a few weeks, you'd be running a mile. A month later, you'd be running a few miles. And then 10 miles, 11, 12, 13, and more.

You will achieve your goals and develop an abundance of confidence in exactly the same way. Sure, we'd all love to have instant results, but that's daydreaming, not reality. Confident people break their goals down into a series of individual actions that allow them, step-by-step, to achieve their goals.

If your ultimate goal is to move into a dramatically different career, you may need to build up certain skills, pick up particular experience, and make the right contacts. You may need to go on a course, sit an exam, gain a qualification or two as well.

If part of your vision is to buy a house in the countryside where you can live a more peaceful life, you may need to put aside money every month towards it. You may need to research potential areas to live, and look at how you would make a living if you were to move. If you have a partner and children, you would have to consider their needs too.

Whatever your goal, make a list of all the actions you need to take to move forward. Start by writing down every action that comes to mind. Treat it as a solo brainstorm. Scribble every action, big and small, that comes to mind. Don't concern yourself about what order you'd need to do them in or when you're going to get the time to fit it all in.

Make an exhaustive list. Finally, look at your list of actions and pick one out that you can do today. If you could do several of them, pick the one you like the look of most. Then do it. Yes, right now. Take that first step towards your vision and goals. Put the book down and *do*, not read.

Action before confidence

Congratulations if you put the book down and did something – if you managed to take that first action. You're part of an elite minority of people who actually have more self-belief than they might have thought.

But don't beat yourself up if you read the last section and carried on reading to this section. You may be thinking that I've sprung it a bit suddenly on you. Perhaps you were hoping there'd be a few more exercises to help you build up your confidence before you actually had to *do* anything.

The truth is that setting goals and listing actions are a great start – but they aren't enough. Your confidence grows as a result of your actions, not intentions. Lots of people have good intentions. How many times have you heard friends saying 'I wish I could lose weight' or 'I need to get a new job' or 'I wish I could give up smoking' or 'I'd love to run my own business' or the many other deeds people *intend* to do? But unless an intention is turned into an action, it's really only a thought in someone's head (or words on a sheet of paper).

People sometimes wait to 'feel confident' before taking action. But that isn't how it works, I'm afraid. Action precedes confidence – not the other way around. Taking action will make you feel confident. Wait to feel more confident before taking action and it will probably never come.

Remember the notion that what we *do, think,* and *feel* are interlinked. As it happens, most people find it harder to change how they feel than to change how they behave. So avoid waiting around for the confidence to arrive from nowhere, because it won't.

Back in Chapter 1, I defined confidence as 'the ability to take appropriate and effective action, however challenging it may feel at the time'. Most people feel a little scared when they take on new challenges. But you can kill those anxious feelings by taking action. Take even a small action and you feel a little more confident. Take another action and that feeling of confidence swells still further. Do it again and again and your initial successes pave the way for larger ones. Make no mistake: you may not be confident when you start, but you have to start to be confident.

"Success seems to be connected with action. Successful people keep moving."

Conrad Hilton Sr, hotelier

That first action

Kick off with even the tiniest action and you may find that it generates its own momentum. If a task is daunting, tell yourself that you will do it for five minutes today. Come on, a mere five minutes. There are 24 hours in the day and all you need to commit right now is one-twelfth of one hour. That still leaves you with 287 other twelfths-of-an-hour to do whatever else you feel like doing!

If you're on the lookout for a new job, dig out your old CV and scribble some notes on the bits you'll change. Spend a few minutes on it today and your subconscious mind can work on it overnight. If you want to get into better physical shape, at least change into your workout clothes and go for a brisk walk today if you can't face the gym until tomorrow. Even a few minutes of action today is better than nothing until tomorrow.

The point is simply *to begin*. You will feel better about your task and yourself immediately. Who knows? You might even enjoy it and find yourself doing it for another five minutes.

But even if you only last that first five minutes, congratulate yourself. Smiling is free, so give yourself a big smile. And tell yourself – perhaps quietly in your head if you're surrounded by people – how proud you are that you have followed through with your first action towards achieving your goals. When I'm sat at my desk and I feel good about what I've achieved, I sometimes do whoop and clap or get up and do a funky dance. You may think that's stupid, but hell, it makes me feel good!

But enough about what I do. What could *you* do right now? Rather than reading on to the next section of this book, what could you do right now – for just five minutes?

"A good plan vigorously executed right now is far better than a perfect plan executed next week."

George S. Patton, US General

Building momentum

They say that the devil is in the detail. And I think the saying means that if you overlook some of the details of a plan, things could all go horribly wrong.

I prefer to say that the angel is in the detail. Because when it comes to turning your intentions into reality, thinking through your actions in more detail means you will be more ready to succeed.

Psychologists make a distinction between plain old intentions and *implementation* intentions. We class the two separately because we know from decades of research and many studies that people who plan at the implementation level are much more likely to carry out their intentions.

An implementation intention is the fleshed-out version of the actions you listed to achieve your goal. It is detailed in terms of exactly what you will do, who else might be involved, where it will happen, and when it will happen.

Say you want to get in shape and have set yourself a goal to do 20 push-ups and 40 sit-ups every day. Rather than just promise you're going to do it every day, you can help yourself to succeed by thinking through exactly how you will make it happen. Will you do it in the morning by dropping to the floor right next to your bed? How about in the kitchen while the kettle is boiling for your first cup of coffee for the day? Or in the evening in front of the television while you're watching your favourite show?

Honestly, taking that little extra time to think through the details of your plan can make all the difference. Here's the science bit. Professors Peter Gollwitzer and Veronika Brandstätter studied a group of students who had to write an essay on how they spent Christmas Eve. But the twist was that the students had to submit their assignments on 26 December.

As you can imagine, only a third of the students managed to get their papers in on time. But the researchers had also asked a second group of students to create a specific, observable, and timed outcome, thinking about both when *and* where they intended to write their reports. A massive 75 per cent of the students in this group managed to get their assignments in on time.

The lesson is clear. If you want to double your chances of achieving your goals, take a few extra moments to think about not only the 'what' but also the 'when', 'where', and 'how'. And a handy way to turn your common-variety intentions into super-sexy implementation intentions is to draw up a little table:

Action plan

1 What?	2 How exactly?	3 Who is involved?	4 Where?	5 When?
Action 1				
Action 2				
Action 3 . . .				

If they can do it . . .

David, 33, is trying to get out of debt. Having just proposed to his girlfriend Louisa, he has set himself a SPOT goal: to pay off £10,000 of his debts within the next two years. Here are a few of his actions.

1 What?	2 How exactly?	3 Who is involved?	4 Where?	5 When?
Research ways to pay off my debts.	Phone banks to see if I can get a better interest rate on the mortgage.	Just me.	I'll set up a bedroom office so I don't get disturbed by Louisa watching TV in the lounge.	A week on Monday – when I have the day off work.
More research.	Get advice from Jason on whether I should get a financial adviser.	Jason – I think he has a good financial adviser.	At home.	When Louisa and I are meeting him and his wife for dinner in two weeks' time.
More research.	Look online to see if I can get a better deal on my credit cards.	Rod at work is a whiz at finding things online.	On my work computer.	Tomorrow – if Rod can spare 20 minutes to help.
Spend less money.	Calculate a budget to figure out exactly how much I need to get by on a weekly basis.	Me and Louisa.	At home.	This weekend when Louisa is off work.

Fill up your table by working through these five steps:

1 Copy your individual actions into the left-hand column.

2 Think about how that action would look if you had to tell a 12-year-old child to do it for you. You'd need to be a lot more specific. While in column 1 you could say 'Look for a new job', in column 2 you'd have to go into detail: 'Send emails to ex-colleagues and acquaintances to see if they have vacancies for a teaching assistant.'

3 Ask yourself if someone else could help you complete your action. For example, if I wanted to lose weight, I know that a friend has just hired a personal trainer so I'd ask my friend for his opinions on whether I should get one too. We need all the help we can get, so if you know someone who could offer support or advice, take it.

4 Consider if your action would be best performed in any particular location. Do you need to find an Ashram for your yoga class, a library to read up on new techniques to use in your job, an internet café to research potential new employers online, a swanky restaurant to entertain your friends?

5 Finally, give yourself a deadline for the action. While your overall goal may have a deadline of many weeks or months, your individual actions should probably have deadlines of days, or a couple of weeks at most. Put actions on the back-burner and you risk leaving them there forever.

Congratulations. You now have a concrete plan of action. Put it somewhere you'll see it daily. Pin a copy on your fridge. Or photocopy it and stick multiple copies around your home or workplace.

Don't shove it in a drawer. And if you work through your actions one by one, you will soon be reaping the benefits of a more confident, new you.

If tomorrow never comes

If confidence is about taking action in spite of how you may feel, procrastination is its evil nemesis. Procrastination is about avoiding immediate action because of how you feel. Both confidence and procrastination fuel the *do, think, feel* cycle. Confident actions lead to confident beliefs and confident feelings. Postponing action leads to beliefs that you can't do it and looming fears that you will never do it. Avoidance leads to a vicious circle: the more you avoid, the more you want to avoid.

Some people put off making decisions and taking action because they want to feel more certain that their decisions will be the 'right' ones. Especially when it comes to making the big decisions in life, they have a 'wait and see' attitude, hoping the perfect plan or right moment will come along. But often waiting provides only a false sense of security – when it comes to making life decisions, we can't ever know that we've made the 'right' choices. Few decisions in life are clear-cut enough for one choice to leap out as being unambiguously better than the other choices you have. And if you wait too long, you will end up missing opportunities. That job offer won't stay open forever. That person you're attracted to could end up going out with someone else. That house you want to buy could get snapped up by another buyer.

If you find yourself putting action off until tomorrow again and again, you're not alone. Surveys show that around one in five people consider themselves not only to be procrastinators but *chronic* procrastinators. Thankfully, there is a technique to shift how you feel and give you an extra little push to act.

Confidence Booster: Rut-busting

There is no magic wand I can wave to make you do anything. *You* are the only one who can make yourself begin what you need to do. But here's a simple technique to pile the pressure on you just that little bit more.

Time to get your trusty journal or notepad out. If you want to say goodbye to your delaying tactics, write down the answers to these questions the next time you are dallying over a task:

■ What are the *advantages* of starting this right now?

■ What are the *disadvantages* of leaving this till later?

■ What *excuses* are you using to avoid doing this right now?

■ What do you have to *lose*?

■ What *reward* can you give yourself for starting this?

If they can do it …

Julia is a 45-year-old photographer. She has been invited to a get-together of some of her old friends. But she is worried that her friends could be making more money, might be married and living in big houses, and so on. But by working through the rut-busting technique, she realises that:

■ the *advantage* of going is that she would catch up with friends she has not seen in years and perhaps re-establish a few friendships

■ the *disadvantage* of not going is that she would not see them for many years and rob herself of the opportunity to reinstate old friendships

- her *excuse* is that she doesn't feel she measures up against their happier and more successful lives

- she has nothing to *lose*: in the worst-case scenario, she could leave early and it would only waste two hours of a single evening

- as an *incentive* to go, she decides to buy a new dress that she could wear again at other events.

Rather than wait for circumstances to change and confidence to fall in your lap (which rarely happens), you can bring about change in your life. You can grasp the confidence you want. But remember that this is not a book to read and set aside. You can grow your confidence only if you participate, work through the exercises, do the thinking, and take that first step. So what are the advantages of starting your first action right now?

ONWARDS AND UPWARDS

- You can feel more in control and confident about your life by creating a vision of what you would like to have in your life. If life is a journey, then your vision is a picture of your destination.

- To create your vision, imagine a celebratory party thrown in your honour, say five or ten years in the future. What would you like to have going on in your life by then?

- Confident people know their values – the set of principles or guidelines by which they want to live their lives. If you understand your values, you can make more confident choices about what to invest your time and energy into and what to turn down.

- There's a lot of science behind effective goal setting, and it shows two things. First, that you can help yourself to achieve goals if you make plans as to when and how you will take action. Second, that you should write your goals and plans down.

- And don't forget to make your goals stretching and significant, positive, observable, and timed (SPOT).
- Remember that your confidence grows as a result of your actions. Avoid waiting until you feel more confident before you take action. Jump in and *do* something to feel more confident.

04

Behaving with confidence

"If you look confident you can pull off anything."
Jessica Alba, Hollywood actress

In this chapter you will...

■ learn that behaving in a confident manner – even if you don't feel confident to begin with – can actually help you to feel more confident

■ understand ways to use your body language and tone of voice to appear confident and instil confidence in others

■ learn simple techniques using your breathing and the release of muscular tension to help you feel more confident

■ explore the language you use in order to weed out unassertive words and phrases

■ accelerate the pace with which you learn to speak and behave more confidently by identifying and observing role models around you.

Have you ever noticed that confident people seem to project their personality outwards and appear larger than life? And that people who lack self-belief seem to shrink away?

Even before most people open their mouths to speak, their body language is broadcasting messages out about how they feel. Their posture, hand movements, eyes and faces are constantly transmitting bulletins about their state of mind.

You can take control of your body language and send the non-verbal messages you want to communicate. No matter how you feel, you can make confident body language your natural habit. You will look and sound as if you are brimming with confidence, as if you have confidence to spare.

But this isn't about pretending or faking confidence to pull the wool over other people's eyes. Behaving confidently can rewire your beliefs and feelings too. You guessed it – we're back to that *do, think, feel* idea. If you steel yourself and use confident body language, you can start to think confidently and feel confident too. In case you're interested, psychologists call it the principle of retrospective rationality. Your brain likes to believe that you're behaving in a fashion that is consistent with your beliefs. So if you start behaving as a confident person, your brain tries to explain your behaviour by forcing your mind to believe that you *are* a confident person.

To top it all, confidence is contagious. Many people – and this may include you – feel that they need confidence the most when they're performing in front of or interacting with other people. By behaving as if you are confident, you make others feel confident about you. They trust you're going to be good and are ready to notice what you're doing well rather than what you're doing badly. If beauty is in the eye of the beholder, then confidence is often in the eye of the observer. Other people can't tell what's going on in your head – whether you feel nervous or not. If you behave with confidence, they will believe you to be confident and treat you that way too.

However you look at it, behaving with confidence is a sure-fire winner.

"If you have zest and enthusiasm, you attract zest and enthusiasm. Life does give back in kind."

Norman Vincent Peale, preacher

You already know what you need to know

Okay, you may not always manage to come across as confidently as you would like. Happily, you probably already know more about body language than you think.

Over to you

Conjure up in your mind a couple of confident people that you know or have observed – even on television. See them in your mind's eye. Consider how they look and sound.

- How do they hold themselves?
- What are they doing with their hands?
- What expressions can you see on their faces?
- When they speak, how do they sound?

In mere moments, I'm sure you can picture very clearly the differences that confident versus less confident people convey. So let's have a look at how you can project that confident demeanour too.

Every breath you take

A lot of behaving with confidence is to do with appearing confident when you're with other people in social or work situations. But here's a technique you can use to alter your physiology well before you have to give that presentation, take your driving test, or play a piano recital.

Your mind affects your body and your body affects your mind. When we're stressed, we take fast, shallow breaths into the top part of our lungs – we pant. But by focusing on how we breathe, we can encourage our minds to feel more confident. The diaphragm is a swathe of connective tissue somewhere below the belly button that we use when we breathe in a natural way. Learn to breathe diaphragmatically and you can defuse negative emotions at will.

Confidence Booster: Diaphragmatic breathing

Practise diaphragmatic breathing at home by working through the following steps:

- Place your right hand on your chest and your left hand on your belly button. Take a few short sniffs as if you're trying to identify a pleasant smell in the air. Or sniff as if you have a runny nose and want to stop it from dripping! You should feel your left hand moving – that's where your diaphragm is.

- Now take slow deep breaths into your belly, the bottom part of your lungs. Only your left hand should rise as you inhale and fall as you breathe out. Your right hand should remain completely still. Inhale to a slow count of four, and exhale to a slow count of four.

- Do this for a few minutes and you should feel very relaxed. Your fingers and toes may start to feel warm as your body relaxes and sends blood rushing to your extremities.

Practise diaphragmatic breathing and get used to using it when you're in a crunch. A lot of people reach for a cigarette when they're stressed. But researchers Tony Schwartz and Catherine McCarthy found that deep breathing can alleviate stress just as effectively without inhaling a lungful of smoke!

Sterling stances and perfect poise

I always used to wonder in the Superman films and TV shows how no one could tell that Clark Kent was the same person as the man of steel. But a big part of how the actors distinguished between the two was in how they held themselves. Superman stood upright with his chin held high and his chest puffed out. Clark Kent slumped his shoulders forward and kept his eyes focused mere inches from his own feet.

The first signal you get about someone's confidence or lack of it is in how they walk and hold themselves. Even from a distance – and long before you get close enough to make eye contact – you can see whether someone's shoulders and head are slumped in defeat or held high with conviction. Your quickest route to begin radiating confidence is to sort out your posture.

Imagine that a piece of silver string is attached to the top of your head. Now picture a giant invisible puppet master towering over you. See the puppet master pulling the string straight up. Do it right now – whether you're standing on a train platform, sitting in an aeroplane seat, soaking in a hot bath, or even sitting in a chair. Imagine that someone is pulling the silver string gently upwards. Your back is straightening and your head is lifting. The muscles in your neck are elongating. In fact, all of the muscles in your body would be lengthening to bring you up to your full height.

We all get lazy with our postures, particularly when we're tired. So try it for the next few days. Make a conscious effort to monitor your posture and imagine that puppet master gently pulling you upwards. Behave confidently and you will think confidently because your mind has no choice but to respond to what your body is doing.

Get ready to succeed

You can adopt the secrets of confident body language more quickly by identifying role models who are already confident. You may know a friend who manages to be engaging and entertaining at social events. Perhaps you admire the way a particular celebrity radiates self-belief while talking on a TV chat show. Your role models could be real-life or fictional, dead or alive. When I give a speech, I bring to mind the resonant voice and manner of Captain Jean-Luc Picard (as played by classically trained actor Patrick Stewart) from *Star Trek: The Next Generation*, who I think embodies confidence and gravitas.

Whatever you like about your role models, scrutinise their behaviour and use it as a source of inspiration and ideas for how you can behave with confidence too.

Don't be a jerk

You can tell how confident people are even if they have their backs to you. Watch their hands and bodily movements. You don't see corporate hot-shots or television presenters jingling change in their pockets or scratching their heads. They don't shift their weight from one foot to the other or bite their nails. They don't tap their feet or fidget with their hands. And they don't do any of that because moving jerkily communicates restlessness. Fast, small movements look like twitches and tics, shudders and spasms. It's slow, large movements that signal confidence.

Be a smooth operator by keeping your hands still and relaxed when other people are talking. If you're not sure what to do with your hands, watch the confident people around you for ideas. But be sure to monitor yourself for danger signs like:

- fidgeting with objects such as pens, rings, or key chains
- touching your hair, face or body
- sucking your fingers or biting your nails
- and, of course, you know better than to cross your arms or even hug yourself unless you want to be seen as someone who's on the back foot.

However, *do* use your hands to illustrate points as you speak. Body language research tells us that people who use their hands when they speak are more visually arresting and psychologically engaging to listen to. But use your hands only in broad, sweeping gestures. For example, hold your palms upwards and you seem to invite and encourage others to pay attention to you.

Watch what you're doing with your feet too. Especially when sitting, people who are feeling less than fully confident often end up tapping their feet or crossing their legs. Confident men tend to sit with their feet planted flat on the floor with their legs slightly apart. Confident women tend to sit with their feet on the floor but with their knees pressed together.

Learning to move in a confident manner won't come overnight. It takes conscious effort and you may lapse occasionally into your old habits whenever you aren't thinking about your posture, hands, or feet. But stick with it and the confidence will come.

Confidence Booster: Muscling out stress

Ever had a massage and been told that your shoulders and back are knotted with tension? You aren't alone. Many people's bodies tighten and tense up when they are feeling anxious. Your shoulders bunch up towards your ears, your fists clench without you noticing, and you may even lock your jaw or grind your teeth when the pressure's on.

Standing tall is *not* the same as tightening up the muscles in your body. A good posture is long and upright, but with the muscles in your body – and particularly your shoulders and back – relaxed. You should have shoulders that are floppy enough to be able to move in a fluid fashion.

If you find yourself tensing up, work through a progressive muscle relaxation technique in the minutes before your moment in the spotlight. The idea: tense and release the muscles in your body from your head down to your toes, like running through a checklist of body parts to undo knots of tension.

- Tense the muscles in your face and jaw. Screw up your face and clench your teeth for a few seconds and then release. Let your jaw go slack and consciously relax the muscles in your cheeks, forehead and around the eyes.

- Now move on to your shoulders, back and chest, and hands. Clench your fists and tense your upper body as if you were getting ready to punch someone. Squeeze for a few seconds and release.

- Next move on to your stomach. Tighten it for all you're worth and release. Then move on to your buttocks, turning them into buns of solid steel for a few seconds.

- Then your thighs. Push your feet into the ground or squeeze your knees together to tauten your thighs. And finally your feet – curl your toes into a ball and hold for a few seconds.

Practise at home until you become familiar enough with the technique to do it in other situations, whether that's on the train ride to a client or while waiting for the announcer to invite you up on stage. Once you get used to it, you'll get even more of an effect by combining it simultaneously with diaphragmatic breathing too.

Fake it until you make it

Here's a question for you: do you smile because you're happy or does smiling cause you to become happy?

If you think that people smile because they're happy, you'd be right. But research tells us that people who smile even when they don't feel happy initially actually become happier too. So if you guessed that, you'd also be right. Isn't that great? A question where we can all be right!

Psychologists back in the 1970s ran experiments in which they asked people to frown or smile for a few minutes even if they didn't feel happy or sad. Lo and behold. The people who frowned felt sadder. The people who smiled became happier. The simple act of smiling kick-starts your nervous system and opens the floodgates for a bunch of feel-good hormones.

So if you want to banish a foul mood and boost your confidence, force yourself to smile. For an instant pick-me-up, positively grin and beam at yourself for a few minutes. Even if it doesn't feel natural at first, do it until your face starts to ache. Maybe even laugh out loud a couple of times. I know people who keep cuttings of favourite cartoons in their desk drawers or links to humorous sites online to get them smiling. Yes, you will feel odd at first – and I'd recommend doing this somewhere away from prying eyes if you don't want people shaking their heads in puzzlement at you.

Think back to the *do, think, feel* loop. If you *do* smiling, you *think* about the concept of happiness and *feel* happier and more confident. I've heard it said: it's *easy* to laugh when things are going well, but it's *important* to laugh when things are going wrong. So put your faith in those scientists from the 1970s and your faith will be rewarded.

Get ready to succeed

You can help yourself to feel more confident by thinking about how you dress and your appearance too. You may already have a favourite outfit that makes you feel confident. But by implication, that means you also have clothes that don't make you feel so good. Don't wait until you feel confident to change your appearance. Revamp your wardrobe, get a new haircut, make yourself over. Take the steps you need in order to feel the confidence you deserve.

The windows to the soul

Eye contact matters. Whether you're negotiating a deal with a client, asking someone out on a date, or giving a speech to a roomful of wedding guests, you need to look others in the eye. Confident people make bold eye contact. Avoid people's gaze and you look either shifty or nervous or both.

But there's a fine line between eye contact and staring. The golden rule is to look other people in the eye when *they* are speaking. However, you can look away when *you* are speaking. If you watch other people, you'll notice that their eyes flick away from yours when they have to think about what they're saying or when they're describing an image that they have in their heads.

Those psychologists from the 1970s looked at eye contact too. And they found that you should typically look at someone for at least 80 to 90 per cent of the time when you're listening. But when it's your turn to speak, drop your amount of gaze to around 50 per cent. Look for too long when you're speaking and you risk coming across as slightly deranged. But look too little and you come across as shy.

Of course, I don't expect you to count the seconds you look at other people. Simply be aware of what you're doing with your eyes to enable you to create a more confident demeanour.

Sounding confident: when less is more

The way people speak often conveys more about their state of mind than the words they choose. People who speak too quietly get labelled 'quiet as a mouse'. Speak in a high-pitched voice and you are 'squeaky like a mouse'. You don't want that to be you, do you?

"Powerful people speak slowly and subservient people quickly – because if they don't speak fast nobody will listen to them."

Sir Michael Caine, actor

Let's help you convey the confidence of a lion rather than a mouse. When it comes to projecting an aura of confidence with your voice, the trick is simple to remember: speak slow, low, and loud.

Think about confident people that you know. Play back in your head what it's like to be in their presence. How do they sound? Chances are, they are loud and clear. They don't mumble or mutter or speak so quietly that you strain to make out the words. They don't screech in a pitchy voice that can only be heard by dogs and cats. Neither do their words tumble over themselves so quickly that one word crashes into the next.

So, speak slow, low, and loud. Let's look at what that means in practice.

- Let's start with the *slow* bit. Manage your pace. Make a conscious effort to slow down what you say. You can not only speak each sentence more slowly but also try to take a slightly longer pause between the end of one sentence and the beginning of the next. Allow a pause of several heartbeats, take a breath, choose your words with care, then speak.

- Think about the *pitch* of your voice too. Confident people don't squeal or screech or giggle. They speak in low, deep tones. Of course your voice has a natural range and I only suggest that you speak in the lower part of that register rather than force your voice artificially lower than it should go.

- Finally, think about your *volume*. Confident people speak loudly. And you probably need to as well. If you don't believe me, ask the opinion of your closest friends. Beg them to tell you the truth. Could you do with speaking up more loudly at times?

It sounds simple enough. But don't expect to become a more confident speaker immediately. It may feel unnatural at first. You may grimace at the sound of your own voice and feel that you sound unnatural or too loud. But I'm willing to wager that you actually sound better to everyone else. So give it time. You're trying to overcome the habits of a lifetime. Remind yourself *slow, low and loud* every time you go into a meeting, make a telephone call, or talk to someone at a party, and you will soon find yourself conveying a powerful sense of confidence.

Confidence Booster: Performing vocal gymnastics

To help you speak more loudly and clearly, use this fun technique to warm up your lips, throat, and tongue for whatever your main event might be. A famous theatre director taught me it. It's especially handy if you mumble or stutter when the pressure's on.

Find a place where you won't be overheard and practise sounding out the following syllables in a loud, clear fashion.

- **'Puh buh'** – the 'p' and 'b' sounds warm up the front of your mouth and lips.

- **'Kuh guh'** – these two hard consonant sounds warm up the back of the throat and tongue.

- **'Tuh duh'** – these two sounds warm up the middle bit of your mouth including the tip of your tongue.

Exaggerate the movement of your lips and face so you can feel the muscles working. Ideally, do it in front of a mirror so you can see your lips and face moving. Start softly on one of the pair of syllables and repeat it at least a dozen times (e.g. 'puh buh, puh buh, puh buh . . .' and so on), getting slightly louder each time until you are almost spitting the sounds out.

Remember to breathe diaphragmatically as well. Taking deep breaths into your belly will help you to speak with more volume and for longer without having to draw breath.

What are your words worth?

Early in my career, I ran a workshop with a colleague. I opened the workshop and spoke for about half an hour. I thought it went well. But my colleague told me that in the first 10 minutes alone, I had said 'you know' over 40 times. And then she got bored and stopped counting.

I was mortified and really annoyed with myself. But it was a great lesson. Because many people use verbal fillers such as 'sort of', 'like', 'I mean', or 'you know'. Words and phrases that add nothing to a conversation. That exist only to pad out the words that matter.

Look out for your own verbal fillers. 'Er' and 'um' are the two most common ones, but also beware of phrases such as:

- 'I'm *only* the office manager'
- 'It's *just* a hobby of mine'
- 'I *hope* that we can meet up again'.

Look out for 'just', 'only' and 'I hope' – words that make you appear weak. So get rid of them. And think about everything you say. Throw out 'I'll try' and say instead 'I will'. Rather than say 'I don't think', why not say 'I know'? Don't say 'I'm afraid I won't be able to come to the meeting' – just say 'I can't come to the meeting'.

You can use more positive language. After I learnt that I used 'you know' all the time, I felt more self-conscious for a while. Every time I said 'you know', my inner critic reared up and made me feel stupid. But it got better. By taking a deliberate pause before speaking and making a conscious effort to choose my words with more care, I drove the dreaded phrase from my vocabulary.

Ask a friend to lend a hand in eliminating unassertive words and phrases from your language. Tell your confidant to observe you the next time you speak – perhaps in a meeting at work or a social situation with friends. Afterwards, ask for feedback on any words and phrases that may signal a lack of confidence. Learn what you do wrong and you can start getting it right.

If they can do it ...

Donald, 55, is a regional director for a high street bank. He is responsible for over 400 bank branches and nearly 6,000 staff. However, he came to me for coaching because he felt that his career had stalled. He had noticed that other regional directors were being promoted ahead of him despite them delivering less in terms of business results. He had so far tried to let his achievements speak for themselves, but it was clear that they were not speaking strongly enough. After some discussion, we agreed that he needed to do more to raise his profile and build stronger relationships with the most senior people within the bank who could promote him.

He started observing his colleagues to identify how people behaved to promote themselves. He became aware of key behaviours that he could engage in to help his achievements get noticed.

One key behaviour was simply to speak up more in meetings. He noticed that the colleagues who spoke up most in team meetings seemed to gain favour with the senior managers. Almost regardless of the value of their contributions, the mere act of speaking up was held in high regard by the people who mattered. So he set a goal to speak up more during meetings. As someone who did not always have the confidence to speak spontaneously, he scrutinised how other people spoke. He started taking time before meetings to prepare possible comments and questions that he could raise seemingly off-the-cuff.

He also noticed that many of his peers were more active in visiting the bank's head office in London. He tended to travel to the head office only when it was strictly necessary. Yet he discovered that many of his counterparts were travelling even longer distances than he had to, under the pretext of updating their bosses on what they were doing, but perhaps more importantly, building interpersonal relationships.

By making a handful of simple changes to his behaviour, Donald feels confident that he is a strong contender for promotion when it next becomes available.

Translating your understanding into actions

You get the idea about behaving with confidence. But how about the practice?

Changing your behaviour is both incredibly simple and surprisingly tough. It's simple in that it's easy to understand. Standing up straighter or speaking more loudly is not difficult in the same way that performing complex calculations in your head is difficult. But it's tough in the same way that changing any habit is.

Think about giving up smoking. The theory is simple enough. You throw the cigarettes in the bin and never pick 'em up again. But so many people struggle to give up cigarettes because they have become used to picking up a cigarette first thing in the morning, or having one with a coffee or a beer with friends.

And the same goes for the ingrained habits that may in the past have led you to speak or behave in a less-than-confident manner. The concepts behind what you need to do from now on are easy to grasp. But it takes constant vigilance on your part to make these new habits stick. If you want to get better at behaving with confidence, you need to practise it. Do it again and again. Then again and again some more.

Over to you

Some people make the mistake of trying to do too many things at once when working on confident body language. Better to work on a few behaviours and master them completely before moving on to other ones. So what *three* behaviours are you going to work on to begin with?

▪ . . . .

▪ . . . .

▪ . . . .

If behaving with confidence when socialising or being more assertive with people you love is your objective, set yourself a SPOT goal to conquer that skill. Likewise if your challenge is behaving with confidence when networking or selling to clients or speaking in public or anything else.

Set yourself goals that are Stretching and significant, Positive, Observable, and Timed to ensure you make progress towards becoming the new, more confident you. With effort and persistence on your side, you can achieve whatever you want.

ONWARDS AND UPWARDS

▪ Learning to behave with confidence is often half of the battle when it comes to becoming more confident. Behave in a confident manner and – even if you don't feel confident at first – you can help to rewire how you think and feel about yourself.

▪ Your posture sends secret messages to other people about how you feel. Imagine that you have a piece of silver string attached to the top of your head that is constantly pulling you to stand up straight, tall, and proud.

- Look around you to identify confident people. Make a mental note of what they seem to say or do – what can you learn from them and incorporate into your own repertoire of behaviour?

- Practise the diaphragmatic breathing and muscular relaxation techniques until you are able to wind down your body at will.

- Don't expect results overnight. Remember that it takes practice and a bit of patience to unlearn bad habits and adopt new ones.

05

Dealing confidently with setbacks

"What is the difference between an obstacle and an opportunity? Our attitude toward it. Every opportunity has a difficulty and every difficulty has an opportunity."

J. Sidlow Baxter, theologian

In this chapter you will...

- come to appreciate that *everyone* experiences temporary setbacks and that adversity is a necessary part of personal growth
- train yourself to treat setbacks as obstacles to be overcome rather than indications to give up
- discover ways to deal with the emotional fallout of difficult situations
- apply techniques to find novel and effective ways to tackle problems
- learn to look for the positives in every situation.

Everyone experiences setbacks and difficulties. Hardly anyone ever gets what they want on the first attempt. Even the most talented candidates sometimes get rejected from job interviews. Lively, sociable people get turned down for dates. And entrepreneurs often get turned away dozens or even hundreds of times from potential investors and customers. Such knock-backs could dent your self-confidence – but only if you let them.

And then there are the unexpected challenges that life can throw at us such as redundancy, unforeseen relationship troubles, ill-health, or other sudden changes in circumstance. Again, such events could make us feel badly about ourselves and want to retreat from the world, but it doesn't have to be that way.

The question isn't whether you'll experience setbacks and difficulties. Everyone does. It's whether you'll grow stronger and learn from them. And in this chapter I tell you how.

From setback to superstar success

Let's look at some famous 'failures'.

James Dyson wanted to create a new type of vacuum cleaner. He made 5,127 attempts before he succeeded in creating a working prototype of the bag-less vacuum cleaner that is now the best-selling vacuum cleaner in the world. Do you think he ever felt down? Of course. But he carried on anyway.

Kelly Holmes had a running career blighted by numerous injuries – the British press weren't kind and were quick to label her a failure. She felt so low at times she even cut herself with a pair of scissors. But she won two Olympic gold medals in 2004.

Winston Churchill was defeated in every election for public office for most of his career. It wasn't until he was 62 years old that he was finally elected prime minister.

'Queen of Pop' Madonna didn't hit the big time for years. While going for countless auditions, she had to work in a doughnut shop to pay her way. Being rejected time and time again by record producers who told her that she couldn't sing, she could easily have given up. But she didn't.

Nobody gets it right *all* of the time – not even famous entrepreneurs, sports people, entertainers, and world leaders. If you fail to get the result you want, tell yourself that 'you can't win them all' and then figure out what you could do right next time instead.

"There is no such thing as failure, only feedback."

Robert Allen, writer

You have a choice

Suppose you get passed over for promotion or your proposal for funding gets turned down. Or you go on a date and afterwards your date doesn't return your calls. You've been practising for months but you don't make the team for the big game. How would you feel? Would you be tempted to give up?

Confident people experience setbacks, get rejected, dropped, turned down, dumped, and look foolish. But they don't let it get the better of them. When they don't get the result they want, they try again or try something new. They get knocked down again and again, but they get up again and again. They learn from their situations and decide to forge on regardless. They see setbacks, rejection, and adversity as obstacles to be conquered rather than barriers that can't be surmounted.

You can adopt this confident perspective too. Of course you may sometimes *feel* down or *feel* like giving up. But remember: *do, think, feel.* You can choose to *do* something rather than be overcome by how you feel. Choose to *do* something that overrides how you feel; don't let your feelings determine what you do.

"If you are going through hell, keep going."

Winston Churchill, former prime minister

Get ready to succeed

By all means say 'I failed at this task' but never say 'I'm a failure'. Confident people remember that failure does not make *them* failures. You wouldn't call your friends names like 'loser' or 'failure', so resist attaching such labels to yourself. See a setback as a temporary situation rather than a permanent state of being, a detour rather than a dead-end street.

But you may wonder: what if your circumstances are beyond your control? You can't control who your boss gives the promotion to, or whether someone loves you back. And I say: sure, you can't always control what happens to you, but you *can* control how you respond. When faced with a setback, you can use it as an excuse to give up or carry on regardless. Get passed over for promotion and you could feel miserable and give up. Or ask what you need to do differently to get promoted the next time a vacancy comes around. Get dumped and you could mope at home listening to sad songs and refusing to go out. Or chalk it up to experience and get on with the rest of your social life.

What's done is done. Time to leave it behind. There's no point blaming other people or the circumstances for what's happened. So focus instead on what you can change – what *you can do* next.

Over to you

Think about your own life for a moment. List the things you can and cannot control in your own life.

Stuff I *can* control:

▪ . . . .

▪ . . . .

▪ . . . .

Stuff I *can't* control:

▪ . . . .

▪ . . . .

▪ . . . .

Take another look at the list of factors you think you can't control. Are you 100 per cent, totally sure you can't change them, influence them, budge them even a little? If you're certain, make a commitment to ignore them. No point worrying about stuff you can't control. Focus instead on the things you can.

Coping in a crunch

Okay, so how can you cope when things go wrong?

Before I answer that question, let me take you on a diversion into evolutionary psychology. Most animals are instinctive creatures – they don't wonder what they fancy for dinner or arrange to meet up with friends at the weekend. Humans are unique in that we can think rationally and make plans. Or at least we can most of the time. Because when we feel threatened, we don't think clearly. We react instinctively, emotionally instead.

Ever heard of the fight-or-flight-or-freeze response? All animals – including us humans – have an in-built, pre-programmed response mechanism that's designed to protect us from danger. When our ancestors were faced by ferocious predators, the fight-or-flight-or-freeze system helped them to respond quickly and effectively. They didn't have the luxury of time to ponder what to do. They'd fight off the predator, flee, or freeze in the hope of not being spotted.

Modern-day problems don't usually run the risk of being eaten alive. Yet we still revert to our pre-programmed fight-or-flight-or-freeze response. In a crunch, you may start to get angry even if there is no one to fight. You may experience panic and want to flee the situation. Or you may freeze with indecision.

Luckily, you can short-circuit the fight-or-flight-or-freeze response and put yourself back in control. You can respond in a more appropriate and effective way simply by asking yourself a handful of questions.

Confidence Booster: Taking the STRAIN out

STRAIN stands for six questions to work through when you're feeling stressed. Whether a burst pipe is flooding your home or a colleague has humiliated you in public, you've made a social gaffe about the bride at her wedding, or you've just been fired, these questions allow you to take a time out. You can defuse the emotion from a setback or situation and choose to respond in a rational, effective fashion.

- **Scale**. *How big a deal is this on a scale of 0 to 10?* When we're stressed, we often blow things out of proportion, thinking that it's the worst thing that could possibly happen. But is anyone's life in danger? Is anyone going to repossess your home or take your children away? Those are 9s and 10s. So how much of an impact is this current crisis going to score?

- **Time**. *How much of an issue will this be in six months' time?* With the benefit of hindsight, we know that what seemed awful yesterday often turns out to be not so bad today. And what was terrible last month may be but a passing memory or even a funny story to share. So when you're in the middle of a situation, consider how it might look with the passing of time. Is it really so awful that it's still going to be causing you grief in six months' time?

- **Response**. *Has your response so far been appropriate and effective?* Perhaps you've buried your head in the sand and hoped the problem would go away. Maybe you felt furious, or tearful, or decided to give up. Asking yourself about the suitability and value of whatever you've done so far will ensure you don't continue to behave unproductively.

- **Action**. *What actions could you take now to improve the situation?* What's done is done and whether your response so far has been mildly constructive or dramatically unsuccessful, you need to look at how you could move forward. Sometimes failure signals that it's time for a different tactic. If what you've done so far hasn't worked, then doing almost anything else will probably be better. So what will you do?

■ **Implications**. *What would you do differently next time?* Once the dust has settled, ask yourself how you could avoid getting into the same situation and repeating the same mistake. How would you deal with a similar situation or ideally prevent it from happening at all?

■ **Nourishing thought**. *What can you find that is positive in the situation?* There's a saying that when one door closes, another opens. By looking for the positive in your situation, you learn to take a positive, constructive, nourishing perspective on the situations you find yourself in.

The 'N' in STRAIN reminds us to look for a nourishing thought, because what initially seems a setback can lead to learnings or even create opportunities elsewhere.

I got fired from a job once. They told me that I was rubbish at the work and that I should pack my bags. I wasn't happy – downright miserable in fact. But another job came along that paid more and suited my skills better – my new boss encouraged me to pursue my interests, which meant writing books like this one. To cut a long story short, one of my books caught the attention of the BBC, who gave me my own TV series – presenting a show helping people to get their dream jobs. An experience that remains one of my career highlights. But I would never have had it if I hadn't been fired.

Some of life's most valuable lessons and opportunities really are disguised as setbacks at the time. Sometimes *very* cleverly disguised! It may only be with a bit of time and perspective that you can recognise them as the lessons they are.

If they can do it...

A friend of mine got dumped a couple of years ago. Let's call her Cheryl. She had a young daughter and thought she was happily married, but her husband fell for someone at work and walked out. The divorce forced Cheryl to move into a smaller house, look for a new job, and cope as a single parent. Fast forward to the present though and she's a director of a successful business and she has a new love in her life – a handsome skiing instructor!

Over to you

Perhaps you don't believe me that setbacks can often be opportunities. Believe yourself instead. Take five minutes to jot down answers to the following questions:

- What, on the surface of it, was the best 'mistake' or apparent setback of *your* life?

- What happened?

- Why did you consider it a mistake or setback?

- What lessons did you learn? How have those lessons helped you since?

- What opportunities came out of the situation?

- What does the event tell you about the nature of success versus 'failure'?

Forward not back

It's an all-too-human trait to give ourselves grief over what we *should* have done. But it's easy to give ourselves a hard time with the benefit of hindsight. Of course we *now* realise that we should have been more assertive, said yes to that party invitation, asked that attractive guy or gal out. That we shouldn't have blurted out our opinion, parked the car on the double yellow lines, or embarked on that disastrous relationship. But it happened, and that's fine. Time to move on.

The STRAIN questions help you to look forward, not back. Okay, your response so far may not have worked out. But what action can you take to move forward? How would you handle or avoid the situation next time? What is the positive, the lesson learned, the new opportunity that has been created?

There's nothing mystical in these six questions, but they work. By going through the discipline of asking yourself these questions, you reboot your brain. Like hitting the reset button, you eliminate the emotional turmoil and allow your rational, problem-solving mind to take over.

I know clients who scribble the questions on the inside of their notepads or simply write the word STRAIN on a sticky note to keep in prominent and permanent view. Discipline yourself to do it and you will take confident action even in the worst of times.

Making confident choices, choices, choices

The STRAIN questions are a powerful tool for cutting through emotion and pushing through to find a useful solution. However, the course of action to take is not always clear. You may have several choices with distinct advantages and disadvantages to each. Take the new job and you'll have more responsibility and a large bonus but have to spend longer commuting each way to work. Choose to end an unsatisfactory relationship but risk not meeting anyone more suitable. Decide to report a colleague who is bullying someone else in the team but risk being dragged into a lengthy legal process.

"Take risks: if you win, you will be happy; if you lose, you will be wise."

Anonymous

When a clear choice does not spring up at you, you may benefit from taking a systematic approach to weighing up your choices and deciding what to do. Writing a letter to yourself is a powerful technique for loosening knotty situations. Go ahead, use it – you may be surprised at how effective the result can be.

Confidence Booster: Corresponding with your inner coach

Imagine that you are your own best friend. Write yourself a letter as if you are summarising a friend's situation, the choices they are faced with, and the solution they should take. Start the letter 'Dear {your name}' and start writing. Work through the following steps:

1 **Outline your problem or dilemma**. Take a clean sheet of paper and write about the situation. Even if you don't know what to write, just start writing. Perhaps start with the phrase 'The situation as I see it is that you. . .' Once you see your first few sentences written down, you may find that other words seem to flow from them. Make sure you describe both what's happening and how you feel about it.

2 **Generate possible options**. Write down all of the alternatives for dealing with the situation. Even if you are faced with what seems initially to be a black-or-white, all-or-nothing decision, you may find that there are subtle variations on each option. For example, rather than deciding to stay with your partner or leave forever, you could have a temporary separation or stay but pursue couples counselling. A

temporary separation could be for a few weeks if you moved in with a friend or six months if you rented your own place. With a little thought, you may uncover more options than you first thought.

3 **Weigh up pros and cons**. Write down what you see as the advantages and disadvantages of each option. But think in particular about how each would make you *feel*. By writing down pros and cons, you can more easily see how certain courses of action might be more constructive than others.

4 **Choose a small, positive step to take**. By moving away from an all-or-nothing view of your situation, you may be able to identify a small step you can take in the right direction of one of your options.

A common trap for many people is to get stuck worrying about the 'right' option to take. But if you toy with options continually without making a decision, you can't move forward. You suffer paralysis by analysis. By not choosing, you *are* choosing – to remain helpless.

But take action and you make progress. If you choose to do something that you don't enjoy, you at least learn what you don't like; if you make a mistake, you at least discover what doesn't work. Taking an action often informs what your next step should be. Doing *something* is almost always better than doing nothing.

Throughout your letter, include a description not only of what's going on but also of how you feel. Include your emotions as well as the facts. Do it because research shows that including your feelings can help you to find more effective solutions. For example, one group of researchers looked at people who had been made redundant. People who wrote about the thoughts and feelings they had about losing their jobs found new jobs more quickly than those who didn't. It isn't just an airy-fairy technique for releasing emotions – it provides practical solutions. So write about feelings as well as facts because it will make you more successful.

I coach someone who types an email and actually sends it to himself so that the email sits in his inbox, summarising his situation and his solution. A woman I coach bought a pack of expensive writing paper to compose her letter to herself. Then again, the technique is just as effective if you scribble your notes on a sheet of cheap paper or into your journal too.

If they can do it...

At the age of 36, Gemma has a 14-month-old son and is struggling to decide whether to go back to work or not. She enjoyed her work as a corporate lawyer. But at the same time she doesn't want to return to work and end up regretting not seeing her son grow up. Feeling more than a little uncertain, this is the letter she writes to herself.

Dear Gemma,

By the end of the year, Jonathan will be 2 years old. But now you're wondering if you should go back to work or not.

You do miss the buzz of work. You miss having clients ask you for advice and having colleagues to chat to. The money is great and you like being noticed as a successful, professional woman too. There's also the intellectual challenge of finding ways to sort out clients' problems – you don't get the same kind of mental workout in looking after Jonathan.

Looking after Jonathan is a completely different sort of challenge. Of course you love him and are glad to have him. But he tests your patience rather than your intellect. Yes, I think you realise that you need some sort of intellectual stimulation. But what should that stimulation be?

By going back to work, you worry about missing out on his early years. And perhaps part of the reason you don't want to go back to work is because your own mother took a break from her career and never went back. You had a great childhood. Your mother was always there for you. But is that what you want for your own life?

Okay, so let's think of other options. I guess you could quit law and do something else entirely. You like photography and you've become a real expert taking beautiful photos of Jonathan recently – is there a way you could turn your hobby into a career? Then there's retraining in a different field. That would be intellectually exciting but expensive and probably as demanding as going back to the law firm full-time – although maybe you shouldn't rule it out for now.

You could work part-time. Although that would be difficult working for Briggs & Smith as they work with such large international clients who always have such pressing deadlines. So maybe you could leave the firm and join a client organisation where you'd be under less pressure and be able to work maybe four days a week. Another option would be to find a smaller law firm that specialises in smaller projects.

Yet another alternative would be to look after Jonathan for a few more years – say until he goes off to school in two years' time. You could always find some kind of reading or project to keep your brain ticking over. Or you could get a part-time job doing something unrelated to the law for a few years until he goes to school.

Weighing up those options, I can tell that you don't really want to go back to your old job. The work was so demanding. Imagine how little you'd get to see Jonathan! But you do want to go back to work. You love Jonathan but you don't want to invest all of your energy bringing him up only to have nothing left of yourself once he is grown up. So you do need to work.

You trained as a lawyer and you love being an expert in your field, so it's either law or another profession that uses your brain. Photography is a nice idea but it's not demanding in the way you want – you're not going to get the same mental buzz. And it's probably not going to earn enough money to live on either.

So it sounds like you need to find a job with a smaller law firm where the clients won't be quite so demanding and you can work maybe four days. If you don't like it after three months, you can always try to get your old job back. They've kept it open for you for two years so another three months isn't going to hurt, is it?

Yes, I would recommend that you get on to the internet and start looking for jobs in smaller law firms.

Yours,

(Your inner coach) Gemma

So when can you test-drive this technique? Make a decision to use it *this week*. Okay, you may not have the time to try it right now. But at least make a commitment to set aside a mere 15 minutes of your time – that's only 1 per cent of one day! – in the next 7 days to give it a go. Think about a quandary or situation that is troubling you. Maybe you're not certain whether to take one of a number of options or you're struggling even to see what your options might be. Use the technique and see what you come up with.

Handling the weight of the world

No one is immune from the experiences of loss and disappointment. You can't cut yourself off from your emotions. Negative emotions such as sadness, fear, and anger have crucial roles to play in our lives. Imagine not being able to experience grief over the loss of a loved one, fear in the presence of genuine danger, or anger when you have been treated unfairly. These emotions are an important part of what make you human. They alert you that something is wrong and needs to be put right. To be rid of such feelings would make you a robot – or a vegetable.

Having said that, you can manage your emotions more effectively, no matter how badly you may feel. Because people can and do cope with all sorts of terrible circumstances. Many people who experience tragedies such as life-threatening illness or losing a loved one manage to continue with their lives. They soldier on rather than wallowing in self-pity. They feel as sad, hurt, and distraught as the other people who give up on themselves and their lives. The only difference is that they choose to carry on regardless.

In spite of how they feel, they take action. They make plans, they set goals in life, they get out and carry on with their work and friends and lives. *Do, think, feel.* By taking action, they gradually think differently and feel differently too. By choosing to behave as if they feel confident, they enable themselves to think confidently and feel confidently as well.

If they can do it...

Leanne is a 27-year-old friend of mine. Some years ago, she had pain in her foot and went to hospital. They told her she had cancer: a tumour in her left foot. After a year of painful radiotherapy and operations, she had to have her left leg amputated. She was only 20 at the time.

She would have had every right to feel sorry for herself. To cry and complain about the unfairness of the world and ask for others to take pity on her. But she didn't.

In fact she decided to organise a charity auction to raise money for Macmillan Cancer Support. She convinced millionaires to lend her the use of their private jets. She persuaded local businesses to give her prizes for her auction. She invited hundreds of guests to bid on the prizes. And she raised over £100,000 for charity on a single day.

But it doesn't stop there. She went on to put together a fitness video for people with disabilities. And the last time I spoke to her, she had just signed a book deal to write an autobiography, the uplifting story of how a young woman has triumphed in the face of adversity.

You can't always control what happens to you, but you can control how you respond.

The STRAIN questions are a great way for coping with adversity. And writing yourself a letter is useful if you're stuck for a solution. But sometimes you're not looking for an answer. Just a way to feel better.

You'd like to move on since you got dumped, had that illness, got fired. Or you're already trying to get on with your life. But you still feel too upset, angry, afraid, ashamed, guilty, whatever. The emotions are too strong, they feel overwhelming. Perhaps you need a couple of days as a time out.

To ensure that those couple of days don't stretch on into many days and weeks, you can use this next technique to accelerate your emotional recovery. Rather than be the casualty of your emotions, you can help yourself to feel better. Even if you can't bring yourself to get back out into the real world, you can at least put pen to paper.

Confidence Booster: Expressing negative emotions away

Expressive writing is a potent tool for easing the burden of negative emotions. You aren't looking for an answer – you just want to feel better as quickly as you can. To get the most out of it, you will need to repeat this technique for 30 minutes for between three and five consecutive days.

Choose a time and place in which you can concentrate for half an hour, free from distractions. Then spend the first 15 to 20 minutes writing (or typing) about how you *feel*. This isn't about finding a solution – just your feelings. You must include in your writing two topics:

- the difficult experience or emotional issue that is affecting you

- your vision and goals in life moving forward (and here it may help you to think back to your vision and goals from Chapter 3).

Really let go and explore your deepest emotions and thoughts. You are writing this for no one but yourself, so be totally honest no matter what you may be thinking and feeling. Don't worry about spelling, grammar, or sentence structure. The only rule is that once you begin writing, you continue for at least 15 minutes (or longer if you wish).

Rather than write into the journal you usually use, take separate sheets of paper or a fresh document on your computer. Once you have finished writing, you may wish to seal them away in a box or envelope, symbolically distancing yourself from the difficult experience and the emotions that go with it.

However, here's a health warning: you may actually feel worse immediately after writing about your feelings. Research shows that the benefits of expressive writing can take a couple of days to kick in. So an important final step is to spend your last 10 minutes running through the 'three good things' technique (see 'Confidence Booster: Developing your sense of optimism' on page 48). Turn your attention to whatever you feel grateful for in order to pick up your mood again. And remember that you need to repeat this technique for three to five days to get the most from it.

Research shows that expressive writing has helped people to cope more quickly and effectively with all manner of testing situations including divorce, sexual abuse, and job loss. Studies have even shown that people who capture their most traumatic experiences in writing also make fewer visits to the doctor *and* have lower blood pressure. Expressive writing improves psychological well-being and physical health too.

No matter how badly you may feel, you have a choice. You can let your circumstances get the better of you. Or you can forge on, take action, at least capture your thoughts on paper, *do* something. Which will you choose?

ONWARDS AND UPWARDS

- Setbacks are inevitable stepping stones on the way to eventual success. Confident people get knocked down but keep, keep, keep getting back up again.

- To experience negative emotions is an essential part of being human. The fight-or-flight-or-freeze response has a vital protective function in keeping you alive.

- We all react emotionally rather than rationally when we feel in a pinch. However, you can make better decisions about how to respond by slowing things down. Use the STRAIN questions to take a deliberate time out.

- Write about your situations and emotions if you want to find solutions and to feel better. Something happens between getting your thoughts out of your head and on to paper – it really can help.

- Remember that you always have a choice. Even if you can't control your circumstances, you can choose how you respond. The best way to cope with a setback and escape the funk of dejection is to do something. Don't wait until you feel better to take action. Take action to feel better.

- And it's so important that I'll say it again: the sooner you take action to change your circumstances, the sooner you will feel better about yourself.

Drawing on your resources

"Few men during their lifetime come anywhere near exhausting the resources dwelling in them."

Richard Evelyn Byrd, polar explorer

In this chapter you will...

- identify the unique resources that allow you to recharge your confidence batteries

- consider how people in your life can support, encourage, and advise you

- make a list of your past accomplishments and successes to remind you of all that you have achieved and all that you can still achieve in the future

- discover the skill of mindfulness as a way of banishing worry

- learn – or more likely remind yourself of – the importance of looking after both body and mind

- appreciate the best times of day for you to take on challenging activities.

You can look forward to having some great, confidence-filled days. As you make progress towards your goals, you are certain to achieve more and feel stronger than you have before. However, your mood and confidence may still ebb and flow from day to day. A run of good days may be punctuated by the occasional bad one. Perhaps you have an argument with someone at work, receive a critical comment from someone, or find that your computer has deleted an important file. We all experience problems, conflicts, and nuisances that can leave us feeling anything from angry and wanting to scream to deflated or downright sad.

Fortunately we all have personal sources of strength that we can draw upon to boost our mood and replenish our confidence. Rather than let your feelings get the better of you, you can take action to restore your confidence. By reviewing thoroughly the full range of resources at your disposal, you can recharge your batteries at will. Learn to restore and maintain your confidence in even the toughest of times.

You are one of a kind

Different people draw their strength from different sources. When I have a bad day, I go to the gym and throw weights around. My better half bakes muffins. A good friend shoves himself under the bonnet of a classic car with an oily rag. A client of mine builds her own computers.

What might your resources include? A few of your resources such as your closest friends or most cherished possessions may be sources of strength that are common to many people. But you may have ones that are unique to you too. Consider:

- engaging in activities such as exercise, cooking, having a hot bath, singing
- focusing on your spirituality or faith
- immersing yourself in art or music
- spending time with people
- recollecting positive experiences from the past
- visiting special places
- reading books, inspirational quotations, or stories about historical figures.

You may have a favourite few resources that you habitually draw upon. Perhaps you immerse yourself in a 'boxercise' or Pilates class, press play on your favourite DVD, rustle up a gourmet meal. Maybe you ease into a hot bath lit by scented candles, shoot aliens in an online computer game, or pick up the phone to a friend.

But it's important not to rely on the same old resources all of the time. Because some resources can help you feel good in different ways or at different times. The point of this next exercise is to figure out the full range of rituals, activities, and other sources of strength that you could use. When you feel battered or down, what are the many different and unique ways you could help yourself to recover?

Take Action: Tapping your reserves of confidence

Write down the ways in which you help yourself to feel better or unwind. Simply take the phrase 'I feel good when I...' and complete it as many times as you can. Don't discount any of the ideas that pop into your head. And the more specific you can be, the more you help yourself to feel better when you're not feeling at your best.

You may wish to complete this exercise over several days or even weeks. If you leave it to one side for a while, you may find that other ideas gradually percolate through from your subconscious.

Once you've completed your list, consider which are constructive ways to feel better about yourself and which are less so. For example, even though having *one* scoop of ice cream may be a great way to unwind, does having *three* scoops every night still constitute a productive way to feel better?

Keep and treasure this list as a little catalogue of the ways in which you can manage your emotions and maintain your confidence.

Your turn. This will take you mere seconds to begin drawing up your list of resources. Grab a pen and complete these three phrases to begin with.

■ I feel good when I ....

....

■ I feel good when I ....

....

■ I feel good when I ....

....

If they can do it...

Adam, 46, is a freelance television producer who recently got divorced. He loves his job but finds the ups and downs of his work very demanding. When he's between contracts, he worries about earning enough to pay the bills. When he is working, he puts in long hours and has to deal with the demands of picky executive producers and diva-like actors. To help him cope with both his work stress and the scary prospect of meeting new people and dating again, he writes a list of his resources, completing the phrase 'I feel good when I...' Here are the first 10 items that he thinks of:

- ... spend time with my two children – especially playing football in the garden, helping them with their homework or teaching them to cook us a meal.

- ... listen to music – particularly Madeleine Peyroux when I need to calm down. And tracks like 'Supermassive black hole' by Muse and 'I predict a riot' by Kaiser Chiefs when I need more energy.

- ... cycle through the park – especially late evenings when the park is dark and quiet.

- ... laugh while watching *The Simpsons* and *Family Guy* DVDs.

- ... grind coffee beans and make a fresh pot of coffee. Although when I'm away from home, a double shot of extra-hot latte does the job too!

- ... do 30 press-ups in the morning.

- ... talk things over with Chris. Even if it's only a quick conversation by telephone or instant message, I can rely on him to talk some sense into me when I'm being daft.

- ... phone dad and 'talk' to the dogs. Something about hearing them barking in the background makes me grin like crazy.

■ ... read dark thrillers by Kathy Reichs and Lee Child but also quick reads by James Patterson, David Baldacci, or anyone who writes like them.

■ ... discuss the latest match results with anyone who has an opinion.

Once you have your list of resources, be sure to draw upon them regularly. Create time for yourself to use them – perhaps first thing in the morning, straight after you get home from work or last thing at night. Sure, you may have a lot of work on or responsibilities at home that make it a struggle to find the time. But what about your responsibility to yourself?

Even if it's only a 10-minute break you can claw out for yourself in the middle of a busy day, make it a habit to replenish your energy and confidence on a daily basis. Do it and you can rest assured that you can get over pretty much whatever jagged reality throws at you.

With a little help from our friends

The human race is innately sociable. We need social interaction. Even the most self-sufficient of individuals reaps benefits from spending time with other people. So why take the journey to greater confidence alone? Best friends, parents, relatives, a teacher from school, colleagues from work, an ex-boss, mentors, a neighbour or two – seek out people who can provide you with encouragement, support, advice, and sympathy. Enlist them as accomplices in helping you to succeed.

Share your goals and plans to help yourself to succeed. For starters, by making a promise in front of people you care about, you won't want to let them down.

But before you pick up the phone, type out an email, or drop by to visit, consider that different people are suited to different forms of support. While my own mother is a great source of optimism and unconditional love, I know that she's not best suited to telling me when I'm going wrong or being ridiculous. Equally, while one of my ex-bosses has a sharp and insightful mind when it comes to telling me how to get out of a jam, he's not the kind of person who is terribly good at giving positive strokes.

Over to you

Who could remind you of your commitments and challenge you when you're in danger of faltering? Who could provide you with compassion and commiserations when you're feeling down? And who could you turn to for advice about an impasse with a colleague, a decision in your career, or a choice in your love life?

Whoever you approach, avoid seeking the advice of people who will treat the discussion as an opportunity to tell you where you're going wrong and what you should do. Look for people who will listen and help you to come to your own decision. When you're trying to build your self-confidence, you need people to prompt and support you, not take responsibility for your decisions and make you become dependent on them.

"Friendship makes prosperity more shining and lessens adversity by dividing and sharing it."

Cicero, Roman philosopher

Frenemies and friends

Apparently, socialite and heiress Paris Hilton uses the word 'frenemy' to refer to the friend-enemies that surround her. In a surprisingly sharp way, she realises that not all of the people who besiege her may truly have her best interests at heart.

Not all of the people that surround you may be equally good for your confidence. If people treat you a certain way, you will come to believe that you are that way – and behave like it too. If you spend time with positive people who encourage you, you will feel more confident about yourself. If you allow yourself to be plagued by negative people who put you down, your confidence is likely to spiral downwards too.

Now that may sound obvious. But have you ever considered what to do with the so-called friends and acquaintances that might not be so good for you? Naturally, you want to be liked by everyone. But if certain people undermine your confidence, or drain your enthusiasm and energy, you may need to take a stand. If you are constantly investing more in particular relationships than you get back, consider reducing dramatically the time you spend with them. If any relationships are especially toxic, get rid of them entirely. No matter what your past history with them, you need to look after yourself and assert your right to a more confident life.

But just as bad people can sap your confidence, the right people can boost it. A big part of how we behave is determined by how we see others behaving around us. So consider which of your acquaintances are good for your confidence and could help you achieve your goals. If you want to get better at standing up to bossy colleagues, make sure to lunch with a friend who's already great at it. If you're trying to study more diligently, spend a bit more time with your more bookish friends. Share your goals with like-minded people and allow them to support you. Confidence can be contagious – who would you like to infect you?

Helping our home and work spaces to help us

Say you want to lose weight. We all know that willpower is something that comes and goes for us all. But an immediate action you can take is to banish all sugary and fatty snacks from the cupboard. Because deep-down you know that, in a moment of weakness, you may well succumb to that chocolate bar or packet of biscuits.

Changing your life takes a bit of effort. Sometimes you can help yourself not by changing your behaviour but by changing your environment. If you want to boost your confidence about your body, then surrounding yourself with magazines of air-brushed supermodels isn't going to help you feel good about yourself. Throw out those glossy magazines. If you're trying to do more exercise, then having your gym kit stuffed at the back of your wardrobe doesn't help you when you have to dig it out every time. Put your favourite gym outfit in plain sight so you see it the moment you come home from work to remind yourself it's gym o'clock.

The same goes for work as well as home. If you get distracted by what's going on outside your window when you should be working at your desk, why not move your desk so you face a blank wall? If you waste a lot of time chatting to the colleague who sits opposite you, why not build a pile of books between you so you can't make eye contact as easily?

Your environment is yours to shape. Whether it's to remove stuff that could sabotage your goals or introduce new things into it, consider the changes you could make. Put a favourite photo of yourself on your fridge to remind you not to reach for that unhealthy snack. Put a sticky note on the inside of your front door to remind you to smile and think positively before you leave the house. Buy an extension cable for your computer if studying with the kids in the same room is distracting. Anything to help you attain your goals.

Investing in a confidence bank

The producers of a major TV dance show asked me for help recently – strictly speaking, I can't mention its name. Three of the celebrities on the show felt they were cracking under the pressure of the live shows. Two of the celebrities were famous performers; one was a glamorous lingerie model. And to help them conquer their nerves, I suggested this next exercise.

Do you smile when you look through an album of old photos? Get taken back to a perfect moment when you hear a favourite song? Laugh with old friends or colleagues about when you lived or studied or worked together? If you do, you've already experienced the power of *reminiscence*.

Reminding yourself of past successes and happy times is an intoxicatingly powerful tool for fuelling your mood and confidence in a few moments. Researcher Fred Bryant at the University of Chicago found that as little as 10 minutes of reminiscing was enough to have a significant impact on how people felt.

It's a versatile tool too. You can use it to restore your confidence after a rough day, a rejection, an argument, or whatever else has happened. Or you can use it to prepare yourself for a daunting challenge, a driving test, your first day in a new job, a big date.

Many people underestimate the scale of their past successes and emotional highpoints. They downplay or take for granted what they have accomplished or experienced. But you shouldn't! Jogging your memory about all you have done so far is a great way to remind yourself that you are more resilient than you may sometimes feel. Looking at your past, you will see that you are still capable of so much more in the present and future. You can tell yourself: 'I've done all this so far, I can do even more now.' This next exercise gets you to consider the FACTs of life.

Take Action: Considering the FACTs of life

This exercise is about bringing to mind all of your Feats, Achievements, Challenges overcome, and Triumphs. Take a sheet of paper and write down every success you can think of. If in doubt, write it down. You can edit the list later.

Consider it an autobiography of what you've done and like about yourself. Use the broadest definition of the word 'success' possible. Some of your successes may be grand in scope; others may be smaller and more personal. Think about all of the different areas of your life including your financial and work success, family and friends, education, problems in life you overcame, and changes or hardships you have coped with. Likewise, include personality traits you are proud to have, skills you mastered, compliments received, times you were kind or helpful, ideas you were responsible for, people you are delighted to have influenced or affected. The list is pretty much endless.

You'll notice that there's a little overlap between this exercise and the 'Telling the story of your strengths' exercise back in Chapter 1. I'd suggest that you *don't* look back at that exercise to begin with. Some people who look back at the log books of their lives tend to focus on work-related or more tangible achievements. But your FACTs could include anything that *you* define as a Feat, Achievement, Challenge overcome, or Triumph.

Write down all that you've done in your life and you may suddenly think: 'Wow. I have achieved a lot.' And you can continue to achieve more.

Keep adding to your list. Put it aside for a few hours or days and come back to it. Keep it by your bedside and jot any thoughts that come to mind as you're falling asleep or waking up. Your list of FACTs is always a work-in-progress rather than a completed list because you'll keep adding to it. Every time you complete a task or accomplish a goal, you will add it to your list, and help your confidence to bloom and grow.

Once you start to write down a few answers, you'll probably find that you'll open up a floodgate of FACTs that demonstrate the many successes in your life. But if you find yourself stalling, you're not alone. The biggest stumbling block for some people in completing this exercise is that they tend to look only for major successes. They discount too much of what they have achieved. Your own list will be personal to you, but here are some examples from the lists of other people to prompt your thinking:

- 'Completed 14 essay projects and an extended dissertation as part of my studies.'
- 'I've raised two children who have turned into healthy, responsible, happy adults.'
- 'Getting promoted to area manager.'
- 'Moving away from home and becoming financially independent of my parents.'
- 'Keeping the promise I made to Kate on her fortieth birthday and going on six dates in the last year.'
- 'Took my son to football practice and sat there, watching and

encouraging and keeping him company, twice a week, for five years!'

- 'Exceeding my performance targets and getting an 'A' rating from my manager the last two years running.'

- 'Setting up the wireless network at home.'

- 'Giving a presentation at the departmental away-day and receiving positive comments on it in spite of how self-conscious I felt.'

- 'Buying my own place, doing it up and turning it into my home and sanctuary.'

- 'I feel good when my daughter spontaneously gives me a hug or tells me she loves me.'

- 'Passing my driving test the first time – despite being so panicky I had a migraine and had to lie down afterwards!'

Over to you

Even if you don't have the time to write out a full list of FACTs, at least get started by jotting down a handful of FACTs right now. Ask yourself:

- What are you pleased to have achieved recently?

- When have you been valued by a person or a group?

- When did you act on your beliefs and do something that was important to you?

- When did you have power or influence over a person, group, or situation?

Enriching your FACT list

Capturing the FACTs of your life is a pretty, er, factual exercise. But to help engage all of your senses when you need to conjure up happier times, consider pulling together mementoes and reminders that trigger positive memories. The idea is to enrich the list of your FACTs so that you have a powerful bank of memories and recollections of when you felt at your happiest and most confident. Your list will differ, but consider assembling collateral such as:

- awards, trophies or certificates – even if these stretch back to your childhood, they can often still provoke strong positive recollections
- letters or congratulatory cards from people
- jewellery, keepsakes, or favourite items of clothing
- items from work such as your first payslip, an old diary chronicling particularly good days or weeks at work, the business cards of people you loved working with, and so on
- souvenirs, books, and even fragrances
- quotations, words, and sounds – including music or poems
- videos and photos of treasured moments, on holiday, a party at work, getting married, celebrating a birthday, and so on.

Even once you've assembled your basic box, you should continue to collect items and memorabilia that you can put into your confidence bank. Every time you experience a success or feel-good moment, think of how you can capture it. Take a photo, pick up a pebble from a beach, buy a postcard, write a few notes in a diary, or do whatever helps you to aid your future recollection.

Replaying your FACTs

Now we get to what you can do with your FACTs. When you're feeling in the need of a pick-me-up, simply find at least 10 minutes to relive your past triumphs. Replay whichever moments seem most appropriate. Play back the situation and immerse yourself in the sights, sounds, smells, and feelings that went with them. Remember how capable, content, and confident you felt. Avoid analysing them or trying to figure out exactly why they make you happy or what you can learn from them. Just savour the moments as clearly as you can.

Consider assembling a folder of particularly relevant memorabilia and memories to boost your confidence when you're preparing for a particular challenge in your life. For example, if you haven't been socialising much lately, pull together a dossier about the friends you have made over the years. If you're going on a date, gather a folio to remind yourself of your interests and positive traits.

If they can do it ...

Caroline is 52 years old. She has worked for her entire life in publishing and for the last 14 years has been the editor of an airline's in-flight magazine. However, a takeover by a larger competitor and a management reshuffle means that Caroline finds herself out of work. She feels more than a flutter of anxiety about the prospect of having to go for job interviews.

She applied for jobs and got invited to a handful of interviews. Of course she researched the organisations, thought about probable interview questions and how she would respond to them, and rehearsed her answers at home in front of a mirror. But that's the easy bit for her as she knows her industry and job inside and out. What worries her is that she sometimes struggles to project her confidence with new people. So she decides to assemble a confidence file of materials to help her feel and act more confidently.

On the morning of her first interview, she makes breakfast as usual and spends a half-hour flicking through the contents of her confidence file. While other candidates might be going through a last-minute interview drill, she reads about her own successes. Amongst her confidence collateral are copies of the magazines that she has been responsible for, a handwritten letter of encouragement from her best friend, a printout of an email from her ex-boss congratulating her on a particular achievement. She looks at a photo of the team's last Christmas dinner and thinks about all of the people that she has hired and coached over the years. She savours the feelings as she reads the message in a good luck card sent by her 8-year-old nephew.

Not only does the portfolio help to banish her nerves, but she actually feels ready to give the interview her best shot.

Focusing on the here and now

Have you ever found yourself lying in bed at night, your head buzzing with worries and unable to sleep? Well, you're not alone, as surveys show that up to one in three adults may suffer from the occasional bout of insomnia.

When you've got a scary event – a presentation, exam, date – coming up, your head may be filled with anxious thoughts about what you must remember to do or what could go wrong. But I'm sure you know – worrying about it when you should be sleeping isn't terribly productive.

This next Confidence Booster is based on a technique that has been around for a long time. Zen Buddhist monks have been practising the art of mindfulness for thousands of years. All that we modern-day psychologists have done is taken the best of the technique and adapted it so that anyone can use it.

Confidence Booster: Becoming mindful

Mindfulness is essentially about experiencing the present, rather than dwelling on the past or worrying about the future. The basic idea is simple: to keep your attention focused on what you're experiencing right now without allowing your inner voice to comment on it. To become aware of what's going on around you, but without letting your self-talk pass judgement on it.

Most people find that their inner voices constantly chatter about what goes on around them. Hear a police siren go off in a nearby street and you wonder what the emergency is. See a cute puppy and you think 'Oh, how lovely!' Catch a glimpse of your own reflection in the mirror and you think 'I look good' or 'I look bad' depending on your mood. As I sit writing this chapter, I can hear the sound of the boiler pumping water into the radiator in my office, so I'm thinking it must be cold outside. But mindfulness is about stilling *all* of these thoughts – whether they are good, bad, or neutral. It's the ability to empty your mind of thoughts and create an oasis of calm.

You can be mindful whether you are lying in bed trying to get to sleep, sitting at your desk worrying about something you need to do, or walking down the street. You can use mindfulness at any time that you need to empty your head of worrisome thoughts.

- Ensure that your body is relaxed and comfortable. If stress is causing you to tense your shoulders or putting a furrow on your brow, let your muscles go slack. Take a slow, deep breath. Exhale. And close your eyes.

- Focus on the sensation of your own breathing. Avoid changing the way you breathe. Simply notice what it feels like.

- You may notice your inner voice putting thoughts into your head. That's normal. But now you are going to send your voice away from you. You'll still be able to hear it, but you're going to put some distance between you and it, so that it doesn't speak quite so loudly in your head.

▦ Imagine that each of your thoughts is a car on a road at night. The road is lit by street lamps and stretches into the distance at both ends. But everything else around it is pretty dark. To begin with, you're standing on the pavement by the street. Now, see in your mind's eye the street receding away from you. Imagine that you are flying backwards, away from the street. You can still see the cars driving along the street, but it is far enough away from you that you can't make out any detail about the cars.

▦ You may spot occasional thoughts popping into your head – that's perfectly okay. But simply allow them to pass by, like cars on that distant street, without engaging with them or trying to suppress them. Aim to maintain this mental state for at least 10 minutes.

With mere minutes of mindfulness, you can let go of all the thoughts rushing around in your head. You can hush the internal chatter. Break a cycle of worrying and shed feelings of anxiety, fear, regret, or anything else. Simply let them pass you by.

You can use mindfulness in all sorts of situations – not just when you are trying to sleep or relax. I coached someone who was letting his worries get the better of him even when he was exercising. He lived in the countryside and went for regular runs after work. But despite passing through beautiful scenery, he was actually mulling over mistakes and recent situations that he had handled badly or worrying about the events of the next day. Even listening to music while he ran made no difference as he admitted blocking out the music with his worrisome thoughts. Training him to become more mindful while he went on his evening runs enabled him to enjoy his exercise and unwind more effectively.

The more you use mindfulness, the better you will get at it and the greater the potential benefits. Dr Sara Lazar at Harvard Medical School in the US found that mindfulness training is associated with a thickening of the insula, the brain area that processes emotion. In the same way that your muscles respond to physical exercise, your brain grows stronger in response to mental exercise. Continued mindfulness may help you to grow a thicker, stronger brain that is more able to deal with emotions. Wow.

Get ready to succeed

Learn to distinguish between productive thought and unproductive worry. Sure, if you need to make a plan or organise an event, you need to spend productive time thinking it through. But worrying when you should be sleeping, dining out with friends, reading, making love – come on, that's not achieving anything. A quick tip to unload your worries is to keep a notepad handy at all times. If you have a specific thought about what you must remember to do running around in your head, pick up a pen and write it down. Once you've got it down on paper, you can rest assured you won't forget to do it. And you can focus on what you should be trying to do.

A few of my coaching clients are a bit sceptical when I suggest mindfulness as a technique for banishing worries. They think they are too smart, fast-paced, idea-filled, or imaginative to benefit from it. But the exact opposite is true. Mindfulness *works*.

Take a crack at it right now. Whether you're reading this sat in your favourite chair at home or are surrounded by fellow commuters on a busy train, focus your attention on what is going on around you without thinking about it. Put this book down for a moment and turn your mobile phone off. Close your eyes if it helps you to concentrate (and it's safe to do so!). Simply observe the sounds you hear, the sensations you feel, the thoughts that pass through your head. Do it for five minutes and notice how you feel afterwards.

The squishy stuff that surrounds our brains

The squishy stuff that surrounds your brain is of course your body. And while most of this book has focused on stuff that goes on in your mind – your thoughts and feelings – we can't neglect our bodies.

A friend of mine, a management consultant, is totally focused on building a successful business. His business has quadrupled in size in the last few years but he's always complaining about his health. He is constantly busy with his work and he keeps saying that he needs to get fit and lose the extra pounds he has put on lately. He's seeing a physiotherapist at the moment about a niggling shoulder injury. And he seems incredibly prone to coughs and colds – although he calls them 'man flu'. I'm sure that if he could be more confident about his physical health, he could achieve more in his professional life too. I imagine that not being out-of-breath from climbing a single flight of stairs, not having to worry about his dodgy shoulder, and being able to meet clients without hacking and sneezing, would help him to succeed in his career as well.

"Life is not living, but living in health."

Martial, Roman poet

Your mind and body are not two separate systems. One cannot survive without the other. And no matter how well you train your mind to think more constructively, you will let yourself down if your body isn't similarly well-honed. Even if your confidence goals are completely focused on the work or social or family or sexual spheres of your life, remember that you can't do anything unless the machine that is your physical body is in good shape too.

But I'm not going to lecture you on what to do. Let's face it; you probably already know the kind of things to do. Eat less processed rubbish and munch more fresh fruit and vegetables. Drop the sugary drinks and chug more water. Quit the cigarettes and go easy on the alcohol. Get some regular exercise. You're smart enough to know what you should be doing. You've probably been putting it off and waiting for the 'right' time. Why not make that moment today?

Over to you

What three actions could you take to ensure that your physical body is as nourished as your mind?

▓ I will . . . .

▓ I will . . . .

▓ I will . . . .

Steer clear of the booze and pills

Staying on the topic of feeding your body and mind, let's talk about drugs.

A friend of mine was so petrified of giving the best man's speech at a wedding that he was considering asking a friend who was a doctor to prescribe him a sedative on the sly. I don't know whether he managed to get hold of one in the end. But drugs and alcohol are not long-term solutions; they merely dim your awareness of your surroundings.

There's a saying in psychological circles: 'Feel better, get worse; feel worse, get better.' Sure, having a drink or popping a pill may help you to feel better in the short-term. But you don't learn. Your confidence deteriorates. You learn only to become dependent on the drug.

Plus, researchers aren't even sure that popular drugs for anxiety and depression make that much of a difference. Professor Irving Kirsch at Hull University along with colleagues in the US and Canada published the results of a big international study in 2008. They found that, for most people, even widely prescribed drugs like Prozac and Seroxat are often no more effective than a placebo.

Wow. No more effective than a placebo. So why risk becoming addicted to a drug?

The best option may be to feel worse, but get better. Feel worse in the short-term, anxious, worried, nauseous even. But by tackling the situation, you get better at it each time. To successfully conquer the situation that you feel anxious about, you need to experience some degree of discomfort for your mind to desensitise and get used to it.

Becoming more confident is not always an easy path. But you are stronger than you may feel. So take positive action and remember that when you behave with confidence, you will come to think confidently and feel confident too.

Your tick-tock resource

Do you spring out of bed in the morning ready to face the world or do you become most awake when the sun goes down?

Common wisdom as well as research show that most people can be divided into those who prefer mornings ('larks') or evenings ('owls'). Early birds tend to wake early, prefer to start early in the day, and are at their best during the hours of daylight. Owls prefer afternoons and evenings to morning, and work well late into the night.

Respect when your body and mind are most awake. Think about the best time of day for you to take on formidable challenges. Whether you need to study for an exam, squeeze in a gym workout, or have a difficult discussion with someone, consider when you're most switched on.

I'm an owl. I enjoy going to the gym in the evenings and shudder at the thought of exercising early in the day. I do my best work at night too – I've on occasion found myself working until 2 or 3 a.m. because I feel most alive at night. But I dread having to set the alarm – ideally I'd get up at around 10 or 11 every morning! On the other hand, a colleague of mine is the total opposite. She rises early even at weekends and loves the tranquil part of the day before anyone else is awake to catch up on work or indulge in her favourite activities. Don't ask her to stay late in the office though.

Your body clock is a resource that you can draw upon if you know yourself well enough. You probably already know which part of the day you are most drawn to. So which are you – a lark or an owl?

ONWARDS AND UPWARDS

You are a unique individual and need to decide for yourself what resources work for you and in what circumstances. Once you identify the reinvigorating rituals that pep you up, be sure to incorporate them into your schedule.

▦ The fact that you are unique does not mean that you need be isolated. We are a social species and can draw considerable strength from having the right people around us.

▦ Your memories form the basis for one of the most powerful resources at your disposal. Make a list of your past successes and keep adding to it to build up a powerful database to remind you that you are stronger than you may sometimes feel.

▦ You rob yourself of the present if you spend too much time dwelling on the past or worrying about the future. If you do too much of either, make a concerted effort to focus on the here and now using the mindfulness technique.

▦ Remember that your body and mind are both part of the overall system that is you. A neglected or abused body is hardly going to help your mind to feel at its most confident.

▦ Plan challenging activities at times of the day that best suit you. Whether you are a lark or an owl, learn to respect when you feel at your best rather than forcing yourself to go against your nature.

07

Creating a confident future

"If you don't know where you're going, you will probably end up somewhere else."

Laurence J. Peter, educator

In this chapter you will...

▦ review your progress to make sure you are moving in the right direction

▦ appreciate that it is both normal and expected to make great progress on some days but stall or even slide backwards on other days

▦ take the credit for your successes and make a deliberate effort to celebrate them to keep your motivation high

▦ review the exercises we have covered and choose the techniques that work best for you.

We're nearly there. The finish line is in sight and you're almost fully equipped to tackle whatever challenges you want to take on. Two more tiny techniques to add to your toolkit and you're good to go.

In this final chapter of Part 1 you'll see how to check that you're making progress towards your goals and why celebrating your success is a vital part of realising your confident future.

Making course corrections

Building your confident new future is not a one-time event. On your journey to greater confidence, you need to keep track of how you're doing. If your actions are moving you closer to your goals, you can congratulate yourself and speed ahead. If you hit confidence traffic jams or psychological road blocks, you can investigate alternative routes to get you back on course.

A great way of keeping track is to write up your progress in a diary or journal. You don't have to write much. Perhaps just a couple of bullet points every day or two. Or a few paragraphs every week. But by charting your growth, you can look back and see where you used to be and how you used to feel. You can see how far you've come and keep your motivation high.

Sports coaches, business consultants, and life coaches use a variety of tools to help people measure the ground they've covered and stay on track. I like the GROAN model as a way of checking whether you're doing okay or need to make a course correction.

Confidence Booster: GROANing your way to confidence

The GROAN model is one that I've developed and used to great effect with people ranging from individuals who want to lose weight to managing directors who want to grow their businesses. There are five steps:

- **Goals** – Begin by reminding yourself of your goals. Imagine for a few moments that you have already achieved your goals to jog your memory as to why they are worthwhile.

- **Results** – Ask yourself how much progress you have made. Be honest about it. No point deluding yourself if you're only 50 or 30 or 2 per cent of the way to reaching your goals.

- **Options** – Consider your options for closing the gap between your results and your goals. Even if the results you've achieved so far are in the right direction, ask yourself whether more of the same is what you need. Should you continue as you are, tweak what you're doing, or devise an entirely new approach altogether?

- **Anticipation** – Look ahead to the immediate future. To ensure your continued progress: what possible obstacles or events could crop up to challenge your confidence? And how could you sidestep them?

- **Next steps** – Make sure you decide what you're going to do next. What are the precise steps you will be taking in the next few days or weeks? And when will you do them? Delaying is not a strategy. And neither is hoping that the situation will sort itself out. Make a commitment to take action and stick to it.

"Life is a series of outcomes. Sometimes the outcome is what you want. Great. Figure out what you did right. Sometimes the outcome is what you don't want. Great. Figure out what you did so you don't do it again."

Simone Caruthers, psychologist

Decide for yourself how often you should measure your progress. If you can meaningfully measure how you're doing from one day to the next, by all means work through the GROAN model daily. Keeping a tally of the number of job applications you make every day could be a good idea if your number one priority is to get a new job. If your goal is more long-term, you may wish to review your progress weekly or every couple of weeks. Checking the scales to see how much weight you've lost on a daily basis would be pointless as you'd expect to get fitter over the course of weeks, not days. But you're a sensible person. Work out for yourself how often to review is enough – but not too much.

If they can do it ...

Neela is 23 and for as long as she can remember has found it difficult striking up conversations with new people. She has on more than one occasion been told by people at work and friends of friends that she comes across as disinterested or aloof. She had set herself a goal to grow her circle of friends and has managed to make a few good friends at work. But right now she is struggling to make friends outside of work. She works through the GROAN model to figure out what to do next.

- **Goal**. My goal is to create a group of friends – both from work and away from it – that I can take pleasure spending time with and depend on occasionally. To feel happy and positive about my social life would feel perfect.

▪ **Results**. I've made progress with friends at work, but I haven't made a single new friend outside of work. I've invited people over for dinners, but haven't received any invites back. I don't tend to get invited to parties, and when I did go to that one party, I spoke only to the people I already knew. But I know I'm not the kind of person who shines in a group, so maybe dinners and parties aren't right for me.

▪ **Options**. I should ask my friends what they think. I've told Anthony and Patricia about how I'd love to have more friends so maybe they'll have some ideas. I could always just get better at talking to random people on the street – I know Beth does that all the time. But I think that's too far outside of my comfort zone right now. I could also join a club or society of some kind.

▪ **Anticipation**. I suppose my biggest obstacle is just me. I know what I need to do. It's not that anyone else is stopping me from doing it.

▪ **Next steps**. I'll talk to Anthony tomorrow and Patricia when she gets back from holiday next week to see what suggestions they have. And this weekend I'll look on the internet to see what dance or other evening classes I can find in the area that I could join.

Good days and bad

You sometimes hear people say 'I'm only human'. They may shrug and have a mischievous twinkle in their eye because they've been a bit naughty – but they have a point. We aren't robots. We have slips and lapses, make mistakes, give into the occasional temptation. We make progress one day and falter the next. We have good days and bad.

Some people who are trying to build their confidence expect quick and easy results. But that's not how it happens. You may have days when you make no progress or even seem to be taking steps backwards.

If you're on a journey towards the destination of your vision and goals, you will experience obstacles. Some days you may hit a road block or take a wrong turn that may mean a long detour before you can carry on again. Or your progress may slow like you're in a bottleneck, so much so that you barely feel you're moving at all. But that's normal and expected. The important thing is to persevere, keep going. You just need to think of your growth in terms of your overall trajectory rather than from one day to the next.

In my teenage years, I used to be a competitive ice figure skater, training four or five times a week. Having mastered the single jumps, I was trying to learn more complex jumps such as the double Salchow and double Axel. I sometimes had a great training session, landing a lot of solid jumps. But the next day, I could end up falling many times. My knees got sore and my butt got wet from sliding around on the melting ice. Of course it was frustrating to compare my progress from one day to the next. But looking at my progress from one season to the next, I got better and better.

A client of mine is building an advertising business. One month she wins four or five new accounts. Occasionally she wins none. But to see how she's doing now against how she was doing a year ago, there's no comparison. She's a mogul in the making – she just needs reminding of it occasionally.

By all means aspire to be great in the long-term, but allow yourself to be good or even okay in the short-term. You may want to be a superb public speaker, able to wow audiences of thousands with your manner and wit. Great, but that won't come overnight. In the meantime avoid condemning yourself over the little imperfections in the speeches you give. Respect that you continue to make the effort to improve rather than do nothing.

You are trying to be the best that you can, given your current state of mind and personal resources. So give yourself a break. Be your own best friend. Support your efforts and congratulate yourself for what you manage to do rather than put yourself down for what you haven't quite managed. Because at some point you will suddenly look back and realise how far you've come.

Get ready to succeed

Return to the quizzes in Chapter 1 after a period of, say, three or six months. If you diligently apply the Confidence Boosters in this book and complete the exercises – *writing them down*, not doing them in your head – you are certain to see a marked improvement in your confidence.

Celebrating success

Achieving your goals can be habit-forming. Once you start to see your progress, you'll be wanting, actually wanting, more too.

Welcome to the ride that is the circle of confidence. The more you achieve, the more your confidence grows. The more your confidence grows, the more you'll want to achieve. Get a taste of success and you could find yourself craving more, working harder to get it, and achieving more.

However, scientists tell us that the circle of confidence can need our help. Research by scientists using brain-imaging scanners shows that the parts of the brain that are responsible for generating feelings of excitement become activated only when imagining or experiencing short-term rewards rather than distant ones. If your goal is too far in the future, you can't get truly excited about it. You need to celebrate the mini-milestones along the way rather than wait for the big pay-off in however many months' or years' time.

To keep yourself going, you must allow yourself to take credit for your successes. Acknowledge the work you put into achieving your goals. Because only by consciously recognising your talents, skills, and efforts can you achieve the greatest boost to your confidence.

This step isn't optional. In fact, Professor Martin Seligman and his squad of psychologists at the University of Pennsylvania have shown that if you *don't* actively and consciously take responsibility for your achievements, your confidence may actually dwindle. Without paying attention to your achievements and congratulating yourself for your successes, your mind may start to slip into bad thinking habits. You could start to believe that your achievements were down to dumb luck rather than your own efforts.

Contrast a positive versus negative way of thinking about the achievements you realise:

Positive versus negative views on success

Positive views	Negative views
'I deserved to get the job offer because of the research and rehearsal I did.'	'None of the other candidates could have been much good.'
'I built a great rapport with the client and won her over.'	'My colleagues did all the really hard work in making the pitch to the client.'
'I did a good job.'	'I could have done better.'
'I earned that promotion.'	'I got lucky.'
'I put hours into revising for that exam and it paid off.'	'The examiner must have been in a good mood.'

Our old friend the *do, think, feel* loop kicks in even when you aren't consciously aware of it. Say to yourself that your achievement wasn't a big deal or tell a friend that it was nothing and you will *believe* it too. Make a self-deprecating comment in a jokey fashion because you don't want to appear arrogant and you undermine your confidence. Sure, it may take a while, but it will erode your self-assurance in the end. So don't do it!

Find ways of recognising and celebrating your achievements that work for you. Whether it's a major goal that has taken you many months to complete or a smaller goal that you set yourself that very morning, give yourself credit for what you have achieved. If you put in the good day of studying that you set out to do, take that tub of ice cream from the freezer or that ice cold beer from the fridge and savour your success. Survive giving a presentation at your team away-day and you may want to buy yourself a chocolate bar or pint, handbag or pair of designer jeans. Successes vary in size and importance but by considering affordable and appropriate luxuries, you can ensure you stay believing and feeling confident.

Over to you

Have a think now. What small incentives could you use to reward yourself at the end of each successful day? Jot down at least three gifts or activities you could use to celebrate a daily success.

▦ . . . .

▦ . . . .

▦ . . . .

Confidence Booster: Putting the icing on the confidence cake

Celebrating success is not always about spending money. It's as much about acknowledging your successes to yourself. Some people find it easier to congratulate themselves than others do. If you struggle, try one (or both) of these quick techniques to give yourself the credit you are due for your own accomplishments.

▓ Write down how you feel about your achievement. Perhaps write about it last thing at night to summarise the successes you had that day – that can be a good way to set yourself up for a good night's sleep. If you're keeping a log of your FACTs (from Chapter 6), make sure you add it there too.

▓ Stand in front of a mirror, look your reflection in the eyes, and tell yourself about your achievement out loud. And say it as if you mean it. Imagine that you are celebrating with your best friend and applauding his or her success. If a friend of yours was pleased with an achievement, you wouldn't just say 'That was okay' and change the topic. You would show your excitement and heap praise and compliments on your friend. Let yourself go over the top a bit in sharing the story of your success with yourself.

A final kick in the behind

Building a brilliantly confident you isn't rocket science. Sure, there's a lot of science and research behind the tools in this book. Psychologists the world over have put tens of thousands of people through the exercises and techniques in this book, but the tools are not difficult to understand.

I've said it before and I shall say it one last time. The challenge in creating a confident future isn't in understanding what's in this book – it's in *using it*. Nothing can stop your unbridled progress so long as you *do* the exercises and *use* the techniques. Reading about them, nodding sagely and thinking you get the idea isn't good enough. Research by the scientists I've mentioned as well as others tells us in no uncertain terms that people who skip the writing part and decide only to 'think through' the exercises and techniques cheat themselves and get far smaller benefits. You get out of this book what you put into it. Results are achieved by *actions*, not intentions.

"Two little words that can make all the difference – START NOW."

Mary C. Crowley, entrepreneur

The one-off Take Action exercises in this book provide a powerful foundation for your more confident life. Tick each one off as you complete it and you can be sure you are taking huge strides towards the confident new you.

Take Action exercises	✓
1 Telling the story of your strengths (page 21)	
2 Creating your vision (pages 59–60)	
3 Uncovering your values (pages 67–9)	
4 What do you really, really want? (page 77)	
5 Tapping your reserves of confidence (page 134)	
6 Considering the FACTs of life (pages 141–2)	

If the six Take Action exercises in this book provide the bedrock, then the 15 Confidence Boosters help you to build a towering pillar of confidence. But as you are a unique individual, what works for you will vary from one situation to the next. You may find a few of the techniques particularly effective in your personal life while others work best in your work life. You may find some useful when you're in the midst of a challenge and others more suited to preparing for it or dealing with its aftermath. You may feel more comfortable using certain ones when you're alone and others when you're surrounded by people, say at a party or in an open plan office. Or you may be a person who finds it easier to work with words than mental imagery – or vice versa. As you use the Confidence Boosters, make a note of when they hit the right spot for you.

Confidence Booster	When does it work for you?
Creating your cool CATs	
Giving form to your thoughts	
Pondering possibilities	
Developing your sense of optimism	
Using the movie screen in your head	
Rut-busting	
Diaphragmatic breathing	
Muscling out stress	
Performing vocal gymnastics	
Taking the STRAIN out	
Corresponding with your inner coach	
Expressing negative emotions away	
Becoming mindful	
GROANing your way to confidence	
Putting the icing on the confidence cake	

That's it. We're done. Congratulations.

You now have all of the resources you need to craft a more confident life. If you take action daily, your new sense of confidence is assured. Don't wait to feel more confident first – take action to feel more confident. Don't wait for your circumstances to improve or luck to change. Change your circumstances. Make your own luck. Decide what you want and make it happen for you.

ONWARDS AND UPWARDS

■ Use the GROAN technique occasionally to check that what you're doing is actually delivering the right results.

■ Be kind with yourself and avoid beating yourself up when it comes to reviewing your progress. You wouldn't criticise close friends for all their mistakes, so don't give yourself a hard time when it comes to the little lapses or mistakes you are bound to make.

■ Accept that progress may feel irregular from one day to the next. But so long as you keep moving forward, you will one day suddenly amaze yourself with how far you've come.

■ Make a conscious effort to recognise and celebrate your achievements. Without that positive feedback, you may take for granted what you have achieved and undermine your newfound confidence.

■ Tick off the exercises and techniques as you use them. But remember: reading about and understanding a technique or exercise is not the same as using it!

Part 2

Confidence when you need it

08

Confident public speaking and presentations

Surveys show that more people are scared of having to speak in public than are scared of snakes, spiders, and getting on a plane put together! And I used to be one of them too.

I used to be so worried about speaking in public that I felt physically sick. My stomach churned and I thought I was going to throw up. But I trained myself to get over the nerves. I now give pretty good presentations (and get invited to do so by organisations ranging from colleges and universities to big corporates) and get an enormous buzz out of it as well.

One of the biggest reasons why people lack confidence when speaking is because they haven't done enough preparation – but you have to know the *right* sort of preparation to do. Because a big part of being confident on the big day comes from knowing that everything that *should* go right *will* go right.

Perhaps you need to deliver a speech as the best man or matron of honour. Maybe you need to deliver a project update to your colleagues. Or you need to win over a new client with a clever presentation. Whatever the speech you're giving, work through these seven steps to help yourself shine.

1 Find out exactly what you need to do

Your preparation starts by finding out exactly what you are being asked to do.

- **Who will the audience be?** If someone asks you to give a short presentation to 'the senior managers', are they talking about the handful of senior managers within your department or the 237 senior managers from all over Europe? Be careful not to make any assumptions about your audience. The more you know about them, the better you can prepare.

- **How long are you being asked to speak for?** Don't let anyone wave you aside with vague instructions such as 'Oh, just say a few words, whatever you like.' Get a firm steer on when you should shut up.

- **What is your audience looking to hear?** Consider what the audience is looking for. Guests at a wedding don't want to listen to long-winded speeches all night. They'd probably appreciate a shorter speech so they can get back to the celebrations! If speaking on a work topic, figure out exactly what the audience is coming to hear – are they looking for information or inspiration or a combination of the two?

- **What should the tone of your speech be?** Say you're speaking at a birthday party. Can you be risqué for close friends or strictly PG-rated for the sake of the elderly grandmother or younger nephews and nieces? Speaking to clients, should your tone be professional and formal or friendly and informal?

- **Where will you be speaking?** It makes a difference. If you're speaking in a marquee pitched in someone's back garden, consider whether you'll have a microphone or will have to rely on the strength of your voice to make yourself heard to 200 guests. If you're speaking at a conference, will you have access to a computer and projector or simply be expected to keep the audience's attention with nothing more than a microphone?

Never be afraid to ask lots of questions. Better to get clear guidance on what you need to deliver than be too afraid to ask and give a speech that misses the mark.

2 Engage the passion of your personal perspective

Okay, what are you going to say? Start jotting your thoughts down. Have a one-person brainstorm. Write words or phrases that come to mind on the topic or people you need to speak about. Don't discount anything. Get it all down as what appears a hare-brained idea could spark off a better one.

The longer you spend capturing thoughts and ideas, the better you will feel. As you get your ideas on paper, you will start to see patterns or themes to link together. Don't expect answers to come to you immediately. Just be happy to collect together thoughts, ideas, examples, questions, websites, quotations, case studies, diagrams, charts, pictures, and anecdotes. The more widely you think and read, the more likely you are to be struck by inspiration.

But the best source of material could be *you*. If you're giving a speech or presentation, you may already know a lot about the bride and groom, the community housing project, the dearly deceased, the client proposal, or whatever you need to talk about. The best speeches often stem from a personal perspective. An audience is more likely to engage with a speaker who talks from the heart. Use the following questions to create a unique starting point for your speech:

▧ What's your personal experience of the topic (or person you're speaking about)?

▧ What frustrates you about this topic?

▧ What do you enjoy about it?

▧ What's the weirdest/saddest/funniest/stupidest thing you ever heard about this topic?

▧ What do (or would) your grandparents or a 5-year-old child think about it?

It could be an interesting twist to start your speech with what you used to believe about marriage when you were 6 years old. Or to begin by sharing what your grandmother would make of your company's financial difficulties.

3 Craft your speech structure

Right, you have a bunch of examples, ideas, and anecdotes that you want to talk about. Next you need to assemble them in an order that helps your audience to make sense of them. Imagine if someone presents you with the letters H E P S E and C. Doesn't make sense, does it? But now consider if they were presented in the order S P E E C H.

Think about these ways to order your speech.

- **A chronological order.** Talk about what happened in the past, what's happening in the present, and then what could or should happen in the future. A chronological order is straightforward and you won't lose anyone as you give your talk.

- **An acronym or word.** This can provide a structure to what otherwise seems a random collection of ideas. SWOT is a popular word for talking through strengths and weaknesses, opportunities and threats. But why not create your own? For example, 'I'll talk you through the SURE model – the Scale of the problem, its Urgency, our Response, and I'll finish by Eliciting questions.'

- **Theory followed by practice.** Start with the theory and then describe the practice. For example, 'The theory about marriage is that you find someone you love and then propose. But I'm going to tell you the horrible truth about what happened to John and Laura in practice!'

- **Problem followed by solution.** State a problem, then guide your audience to the solution. For example, 'I'm going to describe the three problems that are causing us financial grief then talk about possible solutions for tackling each of them.'

Don't forget about visual aids. Having something for people to look at while they listen to you is a great way to take some of the pressure off you. Be as daring or conservative as you like – visual aids can be whatever you want. Projecting slides on to a screen can draw the audience's attention away from you and remind you what to say. You could whip out a poster-sized photo of the birthday boy or girl aged 18 months to a round of 'ahhhh'. You could brandish a copy of your company's annual report as you talk about the pressures that your team faces.

4 Practise, practise, practise!

Psychologists talk about the need to practise 'outputting' as well as 'inputting' a speech. Sitting quietly and reading your notes (inputting) pushes it into your brain. But you need to practise speaking it out loud (outputting) so you can pull it out of your brain too.

But I'm not talking about any old way to speak it out loud. They say that practice makes perfect, but I disagree. Because only *perfect* practice makes perfect performance on the big day. The more you simulate the conditions in which you need to give your speech, the more you will get out of your practice. If the actual presentation needs to be delivered while standing up, then stand while you practise. Project the slides behind you if you're using them. Rehearse out loud and at the right volume as if a packed audience is in front of you.

It's up to you how much you want to rely on notes. Read your notes if you need to do it that way – even famous business leaders, presidents, and prime ministers sometimes read out their speeches. But practise your speech enough so that you don't have to rely on notes for every word. If you look up occasionally and make eye contact with your audience, you show that you know what you're talking about. Even better if you can reduce your notes down to a handful of bullet points on a sheet of paper. Every time you run through your speech, you will learn a bit more and need to rely on your notes a little less. If you want to be good, be sure to practise. If you want to be great, practise a lot.

5 Sort out the practical stuff

Having something go wrong on the big day itself won't do much for your confidence. So it pays to think ahead. To ensure that your speech goes smoothly, consider the following:

▓ Do you know exactly where the venue is and how to get there? Don't arrive dripping with sweat because you didn't leave enough time and had to sprint up three flights of stairs to find the right room!

▓ Are you happy with the audiovisual equipment? Do you know how to operate the microphone, laptop, slide projector? And who can help if it breaks down?

▓ Do you know where the toilets are for that last-minute comfort break?

▓ Can you get a glass of water in case your mouth goes dry?

6 Calm your mind and body

Even when we know our material, the voice in our heads – that darned inner critic – can still torture our thoughts. However, the following Confidence Boosters are especially powerful for tackling pre-speech worries.

▓ Well before your speech, start visualising success (see 'Using the movie screen in your head' on pages 51–2) to get your mind used to the idea that you can do it.

▓ If you experience stabs of panic about speaking, use the FACADe Confidence Booster (see 'Giving form to your thoughts' on pages 38–9). Challenge the automatic negative thoughts (ANTs) in your head and you will see that many of your worries are unrealistic.

▪ Prior to the big day, create capability-affirming thoughts (see 'Creating your cool CATs' on page 35) to repeat in the final minutes before you deliver your speech.

▪ A half-hour or so before your speech, find an empty office, dressing room, or even toilet cubicle and do a vocal warm-up (see 'Performing vocal gymnastics' on page 105). And check that you are breathing in a natural, relaxed fashion too (see 'Diaphragmatic breathing' on page 97) .

7 Be entertaining *and* educational

Okay, time to step up and deliver what you need to say. This final step is a reminder that all audiences are looking not only to be informed but also entertained. No matter how dry or technical your topic, you can make it more enjoyable by allowing your personality to come through. So smile, use hand gestures to illustrate key points, and think about your body language (see Chapter 4). If you look like you're having a good time, your audience is more likely to have one too.

09

Confident socialising and dating

Ever been to a party or social occasion and felt self-conscious, not knowing who to talk to or what to say? Well, you're not alone. Many people worry about social situations. And when it comes to dating, there's the added complication of making a good impression on someone you're attracted to. Even people you know who appear to be the life and soul of the party can feel insecure when venturing into unknown social territory.

Most folks would like to meet new people, make friends, enjoy dating and sex, and perhaps find The One. But just because we crave social contact doesn't mean that we are automatically good at it.

Fortunately, social skill is precisely that – it's a *skill*. Professor Bernardo Carducci at the Shyness Research Institute at Indiana University has interviewed thousands of people who experience shyness and he believes that no one is born shy. Which means that social confidence can be taught, practised, and honed. So let's cover seven straightforward tactics enabling you to get more out of socialising and dating.

1 Know what you're getting into

Our fears are often greatest when we don't know what we're letting ourselves in for. So pick up the telephone and speak to your host, or do a little planning to make sure your event or date goes well. Here are some questions to think through:

- What time does the event start and where will it be held? A good tip is to get there on time. Many parties don't get busy until later. If you're nervous about meeting strangers, arriving early means you can be personally introduced to a few people before the crowds appear. If it's a date that you're arranging, ask a friend for advice on suitable venues.

- What do you need to take along? Should you bring a bottle or flowers or some other gift? Whip up a culinary creation or bring a store-bought dessert?

- Who else will be there? Could you bring a friend to keep you company? If you feel nervous about social occasions, find a friend who is adept at social chit-chat to provide moral support.
- What are you going to wear? Plan ahead rather than risk discovering at the last minute that your favourite outfit is stained or hasn't been ironed.

2 Be an active listener, not talker

A lot of people get nervous socially because they don't like being scrutinised by others. They worry that others will be looking and laughing at them. But the reality is that most people are too concerned about themselves to be thinking about you. And you can turn this fact to your advantage.

On dates and in other social situations, people gravitate towards folks who are 'good listeners'. In other words, most people like to talk about themselves. So ask other people about themselves – even the waiter. Once people get talking, you'll feel less tense.

What questions could you ask people? The next time you find yourself with friends, make a mental note of the questions that people ask each other. Or make a comment about what's going on around you – the event, activity, or your general surroundings – and turn it into a question. 'I've never been in this restaurant before – have you?' or 'It's a gorgeous evening, isn't it?'

Of course I'm not suggesting that you fire questions at people irrespective of where the conversation is going – that's an interrogation, not a conversation. But if there is a lull in the conversation, having a few questions at the ready means you can always get the banter going again.

Once you've got someone talking, you can encourage them to talk further by dropping in comments and observations. Show that you're listening with responses such as 'It sounds like your daughter is great fun' or 'You must be very motivated to go running even when it's raining!'

3 Have something to say

Whenever I ask one particular friend how he is, he always replies 'Mustn't grumble.' I've even told him off for saying that, because it puts an immediate downer on the conversation. All I hear is the word 'grumble', which makes me feel like the conversation is going to be hard work.

When I ask another friend 'What have you been up to?' she replies with 'Not a lot.' Again, it kills the conversation dead.

Whether you're talking to a group at a party or a single person on a date, you can't bombard them with questions. You need to talk about yourself as well. Psychologists call it the principle of *reciprocity* – both parties in a conversation have to make a contribution. If you ask people what they do for a living, be ready for them to ask what you do too. But the secret here is to give an answer that encourages other people either to ask further questions or to talk about their lives further.

So avoid giving one-word or overly short answers. Rather than saying 'I'm an accountant', how about 'I studied geography at university but somehow I ended up becoming an accountant. What do you do?' or 'Technically speaking I'm an accountant, but really I consider myself a frustrated artist. What's your secret passion?' Such answers combine self-disclosure, which builds rapport, with a question to return the conversational ball into the other person's court.

Or if someone asks you where you live, don't say 'Clapham'. Try

'Clapham, quite a distance from the nearest train station but really close to a little bakery that sells amazing cranberry muffins'. That contains prompts such as 'train station', 'bakery' and 'muffins', allowing multiple avenues for your conversational partner to pursue.

How would *you* answer the following common questions?

- 'Any plans to go away on holiday?'
- 'Following anything in particular on the telly?'
- 'What do you like doing outside of work?'
- 'Seen any good films/read any good books lately?'

Don't learn responses off-by-heart. But at least have a rough idea of how you could reply to the more common questions that people ask. Just a little preparation will mean you can keep the conversation flowing when you're in the thick of it.

4 Use positive body language

Look as if you're having a good time and you will draw other people to you. Look like you're shy or anxious and of course people will worry about engaging with you. Chapter 4 covers body language and how to behave as if you already possess confidence. But as a quick reminder:

- **Smile and make eye contact.** People notice facial expressions long before they notice your clothes, hair, and so on. People are drawn to smiles – even month-old babies can recognise a smile and respond positively to it. And remember that smiling causes changes in the brain that can make you feel happier too – even if at first you don't feel it.

- **Check your posture and use of hands.** If you let your shoulders slump and have your arms crossed, you send the message that you don't like to talk to people. Stand tall, keep your chin up, and avoid making jerky, awkward movements.

When you're chatting, use a technique called 'active listening' to demonstrate that you are paying attention to what's being said. Nod your head occasionally in agreement with what people say. Use words and noises such as 'yes', 'uh-huh', and 'go on' to signal audibly that you're listening. And allow appropriate expressions to cross your face too – a smile for a funny story, a serious face if someone tells you about a difficult situation, or surprise if someone tells you something unexpected.

5 Be yourself

Managing your outward appearance to mask your initial lack of confidence is a good thing. But pretending to be someone other than yourself is not.

Sure, we bond with people by finding common ground. But that only works if you genuinely share the same passion. Feign interest when you know nothing about a topic and you show yourself up as a fraud.

Part of confident socialising and dating is being comfortable with what you're good or not so good at. If someone asks you about your favourite football team, soap opera, Booker prize-nominated novel, or whatever, be honest. Admit that you don't know anything about it and either show a polite interest (e.g. 'I don't really follow the soaps – do you have a favourite?') or change the topic (e.g. 'I'm more a fan of thrillers myself – what else do you enjoy doing with your time?').

Don't try to be all things to all people. You'll come across better talking about what you actually know and enjoy.

6 Focus your attention outwards

When you feel nervous, you may focus more on what's going on inside your head than what's going on around you. But focusing on what your inner critic says can get distracting when you should be listening to the people around you. However, you can use the principles of mindfulness (see 'Confidence Booster: Becoming mindful' on pages 147–8) not only to calm yourself down but also to focus on other people and away from your own thoughts.

Essentially, becoming more mindful is simply about choosing what you focus on. You probably already do this some of the time anyway. If you're on the telephone but the TV is on, you can switch your attention to the speaker down the line rather than the television next to you. Or if you're at work and people are chatting around you, you can either choose to listen in or focus on what you're supposed to be doing.

Becoming more mindful when you're out and about is pretty much the same thing. But this time you are choosing to direct the spotlight of your attention away from the niggling voice in your head and on to the person talking to you.

Make a concerted effort to listen to what people are saying and doing. Avoid evaluating what's going on. If you notice thoughts cropping up such as 'Oh no, I can't believe I said that!', let them go. Trust yourself to speak without judging everything you say. Research shows that most people usually pay only about half as much attention to you as you think they do. So remember that you'll be judging your comments much more harshly than the people around you will be.

7 Get fired up

Capability-affirming thoughts (see 'Confidence Booster: Creating your cool CATs on page 35) are great for staying positive. Put in the time well before the day of the party or date so you can decide on some positive statements to buoy up your confidence. CATs that have worked for other people include:

- 'It's okay to be nervous but I can keep my nerves in check.'
- 'I'm a good listener.'
- 'Focus on the person I'm talking to.'
- 'I'm going to approach someone and say hello.'
- 'Lots of people feel nervous but I want to enjoy myself.'

Decide on your own CATs and repeat them under your breath or in your head on the way to the event. And when you have finished one conversation and are about to start the next, take the opportunity to remind yourself of them.

Remember to look after your body too. Be aware of your breathing (see 'Confidence Booster: Diaphragmatic breathing' on page 97) to ensure you help yourself to breathe naturally and calmly.

All it takes is a little preparation and a few basic techniques. Soon you will supercharge your social life!

10

Confident encounters at work

Ever heard the saying 'It's not *what* you know, it's *who* you know'? It's true that working relationships play a big part in creating business success. Perhaps you want to state your case for a pay rise to your boss or need to give a colleague hard-hitting criticism about their performance. Maybe you are aiming to negotiate a business deal or simply network with as many new contacts as possible. Whatever you need, it comes down to building effective relationships with people.

Winning over colleagues and clients in business meetings isn't rocket science. As with much in life, a little planning and preparation go a long way. To allow you to be your best at work, I share with you my seven steps to confident encounters at work.

1 Decide on your objective

You need to know what you want out of a meeting or encounter. Do you want to raise your profile in the team, network with prospective clients at a conference, or sign up a new customer?

Whatever you want, write it down. Your objective will help you to keep a clear mind in working towards what you want.

2 Get used to wearing other people's shoes

Business success is about relationships. And to create strong relationships, you need to see all of your interactions through the eyes of other people. Imagine that you're meeting with your boss. What do you think your boss would rather hear – a list of what you're not happy with or suggestions as to how you can make the team more successful? Or if you're meeting with a customer, do you think the customer is more interested in your company's history or how you can save her organisation time and money?

Imagine that you're tuned into the radio station WII-FM. Imagine a big sign on the forehead of everyone you meet that says: 'What's in it for me?' Put yourself into the shoes of other people to answer the question and you will get far. Get used to behaving generously towards other people and you may find that they can't help but help you in turn.

3 Create your spoken logo

Business etiquette usually dictates that you introduce yourself with a hello and your name. No surprises so far. But then you may get asked 'What do you do?' It pays dividends to give some thought to your answer, the 'blurb' or spoken logo you use to introduce yourself. Simply saying 'I'm a teacher' or 'I run a business that creates online advertising' may be accurate. But is it exciting? Does it whet the appetite of the people you talk to and make them want to find out more?

A client of mine says with a cheeky smile: 'I make business people famous' rather than simply saying he works in public relations. I could say 'I'm a coaching psychologist', but that's a bit yawn-inducing. So I tell people 'I'm a TV psychologist'. Even though I don't spend all of my time on television, it's more exciting and encourages people to want to know more.

Think about creating a spoken logo that is appropriate to your audience and your objective. If you want to be taken seriously, you need to make weightier comments about yourself. If you want to capture the interest of people who might not otherwise be interested, think about a quirkier phrase to use. How could you describe yourself in a way that is more exciting than your mere job title?

4 See what works – and what doesn't

They say that there's no need to reinvent the wheel and they're right. Why struggle to find out the best way to do everything when great examples of it are going on all around you?

Look at your colleagues and acquaintances. Pick the ones who get it right most of the time. What is it that they say or do? Is it a phrase or a way with words that you could adapt for your own use? Is it their manner as they enter a room and shake hands with everyone present?

Watch also the colleagues who aren't held in very high regard. What mistakes or *faux pas* do they commit? What do they do (or not do) that causes others to shun them?

People have always learned by observation, learning from their successes and steering clear of their mistakes. You may need to watch other people on a couple of occasions; perhaps capture your thoughts in a journal. But certainly don't be scared to expand your repertoire by learning from others. Looking and listening is one of the most powerful tools available to us to accelerate our confidence in all sorts of business situations.

5 Turn your objective into a SPOT goal

An objective is a start. But in Chapter 3 I talked about how a SPOT goal is even better to keep you motivated. Only when you have a goal that is stretching and significant, positive, observable, and timed can you know at the end of a business encounter whether you have succeeded or need to work harder next time to achieve your goal. Here are some examples of work-related SPOT goals:

- 'I will introduce myself to 12 new people before we break for lunch.'

- 'I will speak up and make at least four contributions in this next meeting.'

- 'By the end of the meeting, I will get the client to agree to us making a formal sales presentation to them.'

6 Forge on

Want to secure that promotion or set up your own business? Want to win new customers or come top of the league table? Whatever is driving you, remember that nothing that's worth doing comes immediately.

The important thing is to keep going. Forge on in the face of the occasional setback. You know what they say: 'If at first you don't succeed...' So use the following exercises and Confidence Boosters when you need a pick-me-up before you try, try again.

- Make sure you're aware of the resources you have at hand to invigorate yourself. Remind yourself of everything you can use to restore your confidence (see 'Take Action: Tapping your reserves of confidence' on page 134).

- In your darkest moments, if you feel really down, use the more powerful writing technique to empty your worries and bad feelings on to paper (see 'Confidence Booster: Expressing negative emotions away' on pages 127–8). Then to shift your attention from what's bothering you, use a favourite activity from your list of resources or check what you've saved up in your confidence bank.

- When you're in the middle of a tough encounter at work, use the CAT Confidence Booster (see 'Creating your cool CATs' on page 35) to keep your inner critic at bay.

7 Review and repeat

Every time you survive an encounter at work, take a few moments to reflect on how it went. But take a balanced approach – consider both what went well and what could have been better. A quick way to review how something went is to think about what you want to start, stop, and continue doing. Ask yourself:

- What should I *start* doing next time that I didn't do this time?
- What should I *stop* doing that didn't work out so well this time?
- What worked well that I want to *continue* doing?

Learn what you can and then try again. Action is always better than over-analysis. So go back to your objective and repeat the seven steps again – only this time even *better* than you did before.

11

Confident job interviews

A lot of people find the make-or-break situation that is an interview a nerve-wracking experience. But it doesn't have to be. *Anyone* can get better at job interviews. No matter when you last had an interview or your previous experience of them, I guarantee that you can do better.

A couple of years ago, the BBC asked me to present a TV show called *How To Get Your Dream Job*. I helped nervous people to do just what the title suggests – to get their dream jobs. Despite their initial lack of confidence, they all got better at showcasing their talents in interviews.

As with much in life, a big part of becoming more confident in interviews is about preparation and practice. When you've put in the hard work, you can go into an interview with the confidence to perform at your best. And I've boiled the essentials down into seven key steps.

1 Do your homework

The first thing to do before an interview is to study the original job advert. Read through it with a highlighter pen and pick out the key words and phrases that tell you what the employer is looking for.

If the advert mentions that the ideal candidate needs to 'schedule appointments for the managing director', you'll need to talk about how you've done that (or something similar) in the past. If the advert states that you need 'a track record of dealing with customers in a professional manner', you can put money on having to explain how you've dealt with different customers during the interview too. Look out also for characteristics such as 'committed', 'outgoing', or 'organised'. You can bet that you'll be asked to talk about why you believe you have those qualities as well.

You'll probably pick out a dozen or so skills and characteristics. Once you've done that, imagine an interviewer asking you to: 'Give me an example to prove that you have that skill or characteristic.' The next step will help you craft your answers.

2 Bring to mind your successes

Interviewers ask pretty much the same questions over and over again. Even supposedly new questions end up being mere twists on the same old theme. So rest assured – you don't have to prepare answers to hundreds of questions. All you need to do is think about your key success stories.

A success story is an anecdote about how you have used a skill to make a difference at work. An employer is ultimately looking for someone who can deliver results – so your stories need to explain how you got things done in your current or previous jobs.

Success stories ensure you make a lasting impact on interviewers. Suppose an interviewer asks you 'Are you a good team player?' You could answer 'Yes, I am'. But does that make you memorable? No, not really. But imagine if you shared with the interviewer a success story that goes along the lines of the following: 'Yes I am a good team player. For example, a colleague fell seriously ill and no one else was willing to cover her meetings. So I took it upon myself to cover her workload. For the weeks she was away, I attended about 12 more client meetings than I usually have. I got into work at 8 a.m. every day and worked till past 7 every night. And I went back into the office on Saturday mornings to catch up on paperwork. But the crucial thing was that I didn't let any of our clients down.' Now, *that*'s a bit more memorable, right?

Invest in a stock-take of how you have made a difference at work. I suggest that you need around 8 or 10 such stories to cover most scenarios that an interviewer could ask you about. To help you create your stories, use the following questions to prompt your thinking:

- What are you proud of having accomplished at work? Why? What did you specifically do to be so proud of it?
- What skills or talents are you known for at work? Can you think of occasions you demonstrated those?
- Can you think of a time you faced a problem at work and overcame it? What did you do and what was the result?
- When have you dealt with a difficult customer? How did you deal with the situation?
- When have you gone beyond the call of duty? What did you do in that situation?
- When have you been a good team player by helping a colleague out?
- What have you been praised or complimented for at work? What did you do to merit the positive comments?

3 Ace your answers

Interviewers often recycle the same old questions. Here are the top 10 most commonly asked questions:

- 'Tell us a bit about yourself.'
- 'What do you know about our organisation?'
- 'What are your strengths?'
- 'What are your weaknesses?'
- 'Why do you want to work for us?'
- 'Why do you want to leave your current job?'
- 'Why should we hire you?'

- 'What makes you a stronger candidate than anyone else?'
- 'Where do you see yourself in five years' time?'
- 'Do you have any questions for us?'

Time to get your thinking cap on – jot down at least a few notes on how you would give answers that mention relevant skills, qualities, or experiences in order to impress the interviewers. So, how would you answer these questions?

4 Prepare to be spontaneous

The more you practise a skill, the better you get at it. And the same goes for giving confident interview responses. Candidates who rehearse giving answers to interview questions always come across better than candidates who don't. This is about preparing so you can *appear* spontaneous during an interview.

I'm not suggesting that you learn interview answers by rote. What I suggest is that you commit your main points to memory so you can deliver polished responses, *as if* you were speaking off-the-cuff.

You can rehearse your answers on your own. Write out a list of interview questions on a notepad then stab your finger on the notepad to pick one. Or write them on note cards and shuffle them into a random order. Read the question out as if an interviewer has asked it and then give your response. Of course, rehearsing interview answers with a friend can be helpful too. Give your friend a list of questions – or even ask your friend to improvise – so you can practise responding to a live person.

5 Plan with military precision

If you're prone to worrying, don't let the logistics of the day let you down. Plan for your interview as if you were planning for a military campaign. Figure out:

■ **What you are going to wear.** Have your suit cleaned and pressed. Get a haircut the week before so you look smart. If you aren't sure about the dress code – business suit or smart casual? – phone ahead.

■ **Your route and journey times.** Aim to get there an hour early. If you're early, you can always kill time in a local café reading a newspaper. Better that than arriving late and in a panic.

■ **Exactly who is interviewing you.** Find out the number of interviewers, plus their names and job titles. That way, you won't have to worry about forgetting or mispronouncing a difficult name when you are introduced to your interviewers.

■ **What written information is available about the job and the organisation.** Ask for a job description, the organisation's website address, and any brochures. That way you won't ask questions during the interview that you should have known the answers to.

6 Manage your emotions

I've covered a lot of techniques and exercises in Part 1 that you can use to feel more confident and in control. But here are three of the most powerful ones that you can use specifically for interviews.

■ Use **visualisation** to run through how you would like the interview to go (see 'Confidence Booster: Using the movie screen in your head' on pages 51–2). See yourself shaking hands with the interviewers, giving them a confident smile. See yourself making good eye contact; imagine the questions they ask and the confident answers that you give.

- To boost your confidence on the big day, **create a folio of your achievements** (see 'Take Action: Considering the FACTs of life' on pages 141–2).

- In the moments before the interview, perhaps while you're waiting in reception, use **diaphragmatic breathing** to defuse negative emotions (see 'Confidence Booster: Diaphragmatic breathing' on page 97).

7 Present your best self

Interviewers want to hire people who are skilled *and* friendly. They'd rather not appoint a skilled but unfriendly person. So interviewers are as strongly influenced by how you come across as by what you say.

Some experts reckon that you should 'be yourself' during an interview. But I suggest that you instead present your 'best self'. You probably don't behave the same way in front of your boss as in front of your team mates, your friends, or your grandparents. So it makes sense to present your most professional and friendly face during an interview.

Think about your body language and tone of voice (see also Chapter 4). Use your gestures, posture, and appropriate smiles. Make sure you *sound* interested and as if you had a great time when you're talking about your achievements. If you're in any doubt as to how you come across, make a recording of yourself and watch it back.

Especially during the first few minutes of the interview, focus on both *what* you say and *how* you say it. There's a lot of truth in the observation that many interviewers make their minds up within the first minutes of an interview. First impressions *do* count. Make them count for you.

12

Confident life change

Making changes in our lives can be daunting. Quitting a job, taking a new one, moving house, entering into a new relationship, leaving a bad situation, starting a programme to get in shape, deciding to start a business or a family, kicking a vice – the list goes on.

Human nature is inherently risk averse. We don't like the unknown so we worry about the challenges that change may throw up. Or we start to wonder if our current situation isn't quite as bad as we first thought. No wonder we sometimes end up doing nothing and sticking with the status quo.

If you need to make a speedy and specific change in one area of your life right now, this chapter is for you. The last 20 years have seen a surge in research on how to bring about personal change. So I can share with you the hard science behind seven essential steps to making change happen.

1 Give it some hard thought

You might know people who tell you to 'just do it', to go ahead and make the change. But rashly flinging yourself headlong into a new situation is rarely the best way to make change stick. Research backs up what you probably already knew anyway – that you're most likely to succeed at change by thinking and planning for it.

Scientists James Prochaska and Carlo DiClemente call this period of thinking *contemplation*, which is merely an elaborate word for thinking about the change from different angles. Their research shows that more contemplation is linked to more successful changes – and here are a couple of exercises to help you do it.

To kick off, start by weighing up the pros and cons of making the change. *Write out* – rather than just thinking through in your head – your answers to four questions:

- What are the benefits or advantages of making the change?
- What are the benefits of sticking with the status quo?
- What are the disadvantages or costs of making the change?
- What are the disadvantages of staying the same?

Once you've identified the pros and cons of your two alternatives, you can identify the actions you could take to make the change. Again by writing down your thoughts, work through these next questions:

- What could you do to maximise the benefits of making the change?
- What could you do to minimise the costs or disadvantages of making the change?

Another way to motivate you to change is to consider the longer-term picture. Create your vision of how you would like your life to look in the future (see 'Take Action: Creating your vision' on pages 59–60). Most people find that having at least a sense of how they would like their futures to look can keep them motivated through the tricky moments of bringing about personal change.

2 Get a second opinion

The poet John Donne once wrote: 'No man is an island.' Of course, no woman is an island either. And there's no reason you need to struggle with your situation on your own.

Amazingly, research shows that even if you don't have anyone to confide in, you can get some of the benefit of a second opinion by *imagining* what someone else might say about your situation.

Imagine you are your own best friend. What observations and advice would you offer up about your situation? Have a think and write yourself a letter describing your dilemma and possible solutions (see 'Confidence Booster: Corresponding with your inner coach' on pages 121–2). Don't worry if you aren't sure what to say. Just start writing or typing. The beauty of the letter-writing technique is that words and ideas somehow tumble freely from your subconscious mind.

Even better if you can seek a genuine second opinion too. In your darkest moments, you may feel you have no one to turn to. But human beings are innately social and empathetic. Whether in person, by email, telephone, or instant messenger, you may be surprised by how willing people are to help. Most people feel flattered to be asked for help, so tell them what's going on with you and see what you can come up with together.

3 Get started ASAP

Even big life decisions can usually be broken down into a number of smaller actions. If you're starting a new job, you may need to buy a new outfit, figure out your new route to work, find out more about the company, meet your boss, and so on. If you're splitting up with an unsatisfactory partner, you may need to put money aside, divide up your belongings, find a new place to live, get the post redirected.

So start getting those actions down on paper. To begin with, don't worry about which ones to do first or exactly how you will accomplish them. Just create one long list of every action – big and small. Change often feels most daunting when it is intangible and unspecific. But break down a big change into its smaller parts and you will see that they can be managed.

Next, prioritise them by turning them into SPOT goals (see the section 'SPOT the goal' in Chapter 3). Think about when, where, and how you will do each one. Keep breaking down big goals until they feel like bite-sized actions that you could take on, one at a time.

To make a successful plan, here are some particular questions to think about:

- Who could *support* you with each of your goals? Who could provide moral support and encouragement, advice, or even practical assistance?

- What could you change about your *environment* to help you make the change? What could you remove (e.g. food stuffs, photographs of the person you're trying to leave behind, etc.) from your home or workplace? And what could you surround yourself with (e.g. healthy snacks, a new lamp for your desk so you can study better, etc.) to give you the best shot at making the change stick?

- What's an appropriate *time period* for each goal? While achieving the overall change could take weeks or months, try to establish mini-milestones along the way so you can keep track of your progress.

4 Ride out the emotional rollercoaster

Another key research finding is that people are more likely to stick with a change when they understand the ups and downs that they will experience. Making change is not an overnight process. Even if you make the change overnight – say by telling your boss that you quit or by putting the deposit down on a new house – your emotions may still feel as if they are stuck in the past.

It's entirely normal to feel ambivalent, confused, uncertain. When you take on a new challenge, you can feel as if you have taken one step forward only to take two steps back (see also the section 'Good days and bad' in Chapter 7). You may make mistakes or occasionally lapse into old, bad habits. Some days you may feel that you've made a terrible blunder or that you no longer have the energy to carry on with your plan at all.

So keep reminding yourself that change is rarely an easy ride. And that confidence is all about doing what we need to do to help us attain our longer-term goals, even if it feels temporarily a bit nerve-wracking or uncomfortable in the present (see also the section 'Confidence is about action' in Chapter 1).

Plus you can help yourself survive the bumpy ride by assembling a first aid kit of resources. Before you embark on your big change, consider how to make yourself feel better when you feel down (see 'Take Action: Tapping your reserves of confidence' on page 134). Like a first aid kit for treating physical injuries, you should have one on hand in case of emergencies. You don't wait until you're bleeding from a bad cut before you go buy one!

5 Take that first step

Making a personal change can feel like doing a parachute jump. Once you take that first step, the rest happens pretty much of its own accord. But we may struggle to take that first step.

Remember that circumstances rarely change of their own accord. By not choosing to take action, you are conspiring with yourself to remain unhappy. *You* are the only person who can dig yourself out of your situation.

The rut-busting Confidence Booster (on page 89) can be a handy way to take that first step. Look over your list of actions and choose a fairly straightforward one that you could do today. If you want to get fit, go for a brisk walk rather than stump up the cash to join the gym. If you want to quit smoking, maybe hold off on the first cigarette of the day until after lunch rather than give up entirely.

Write down the advantages of taking that first small step and the disadvantages of doing nothing. Write down the excuses or reasons you are using to justify doing nothing – you'll be able to see them for what they're worth once you've committed them to paper. And finally, work out how you could reward yourself to celebrate taking that first step. Just one small action to begin with – you can do it!

6 Keep moving

Making a successful change is more often about taking regular, small steps than trying to make great leaps all at once. Aim to do too much in one go and you set yourself up to fail.

At times you may feel that small steps aren't moving you forward fast enough. But all successful human endeavours have been created over a period of time. Say you're starting a course of study, accept that you may at first find it difficult to concentrate. If you've moved in with someone new, allow yourself time to get used to your new setup.

What's more important than the speed of change is to keep going in the right direction. A gritty resolve to keep going, day by day, delivers results. Like the tortoise and the hare, slow and steady beats fast but erratic every time.

7 Celebrate your wins

To keep your motivation high, make sure you celebrate your successes. Find a way to congratulate yourself that works for you. Buy yourself a treat or gift if you feel you deserve it. Even if you don't want to spend money, at least note your achievement and give yourself the recognition you deserve (see 'Confidence Booster: Putting the icing on the confidence cake' on page 164).

People often feel that the achievement of a goal should be its own reward. But that's not how the human brain works. The more you celebrate and make a big deal of what you have achieved, the more confident you will feel about your ability to achieve even more.